Constitutional Politics

Constitutional Politics

The Canadian Forum Book on the Federal Constitutional Proposals 1991–92

Edited by Duncan Cameron and
Miriam Smith

James Lorimer & Company, Publishers
Toronto, 1992

Cover illustration: Paul Zwolak

Canadian Cataloguing in Publication Data

Constitutional politics

Includes bibliographic references and index.
ISBN 1-55028-375-8 (bound). - ISBN 1-55028-373-1 (pbk.)

1. Canada - Constitutional law - Amendments.
2. Canada - Politics and government - 1984 - .*
3. Federal government - Canada. I. Cameron, Duncan, 1944- . II. Smith, Miriam Catherine.

JL27.C65 1992 342.71'03 C92-093755-1

James Lorimer & Company, Publishers
Egerton Ryerson Memorial Building
35 Britain Street
Toronto, Ontario
M5A 1R7

Printed in Canada

Contents

Introduction

Duncan Cameron

On September 24, 1991, in a fifty-nine-page document entitled *Shaping Canada's Future Together: Proposals*, the Mulroney government set out twenty-eight proposals for constitutional change. The initiative was designed to end some thirty years of constitutional wrangling between Ottawa and the provinces. It followed on a decision of the Québec government, after the failure of the Meech Lake Accord, to withdraw from constitutional negotiations until it received a federal offer for change endorsed by the other provinces. This decision was given further force in Bill 150, adopted by the Québec National Assembly. In the absence of an offer accepted by the Québec government and by the Québec population in a referendum, Bill 150 called for a referendum to be held on sovereignty for Québec.

Overcoming the lingering crisis of Canadian federalism is no easy task. Constitutional politics entails overcoming the procedural difficulties that have bedevilled negotiations for decades and confronting very real differences over matters of substance that have produced deadlock. The attempt to strike a constitutional deal to satisfy Québec, the other provinces, the federal government and various groups with concerns of their own — notably the aboriginal peoples — faced the obstacles that have led to failure in the past, most recently in the demise of the Meech Lake Accord. The federal government's response to the constitutional challenge was to place what amounts to a shopping list for change on the table and to signal its willingness to proceed with far-reaching reform.

A constitution is about how a country works. In a federal state such as Canada, it establishes the division of powers between the provinces and the federal government. It is taken seriously by governments because the rules it sets out bind governments themselves. How the constitution is changed is itself an important constitutional issue. In Canada, constitutional change has been subject to discussion by the provinces with the federal government, in a format of intergovernmental negotiation known as executive federalism. Attempts to alter the balance of political power between the two levels of government have been at the heart of the process and of the substantive differences between the two levels.

Constitutional reform has been the subject of various rounds of attempted deal making. The 1991 proposals followed the failure of the Meech round, which itself was intended to correct the perceived shortcomings of the 1982 patriation package. Patriation in 1982 gave Canada a constitutional amending formula for the first time and enshrined a Charter of Rights and Freedoms for individual citizens in the constitution, but was condemned by the Québec National Assembly. In its 1991 approach to constitutional reform, the Conservative government chose to seek endorsement for its proposals from a joint parliamentary committee co-chaired by MP Dorothy Dobbie and Senator Gérald Beaudoin and to have the proposals discussed at a series of national constitutional conferences with citizen involvement, before seeking approval from the provinces. This was in sharp contrast to the Meech round, where the premiers and the federal government agreed to a package of reform measures which were only revealed to the public after the fact, with no amendments allowed. Once Beaudoin-Dobbie reported on the proposals, the federal government and the provinces began their own negotiations.

In past rounds of federal-provincial negotiations, each participant has put forward its demands or requirements and then bargained to ensure that its concerns be met in arriving at what amounts to a consensus. In its September 1991 proposals the Mulroney government refrained from setting out any constitutional amendments that would require unanimous approval. Its goal was to get the agreement of seven provinces with 50 percent of the population, which is the amending formula that applies to almost all except the most basic constitutional amendments, such as changes to the amending formula itself. Securing the assent of the opposition parties in the House of Commons was important to the joint committee process. The government counted on the atmosphere of national crisis to soften partisan criticism and to quiet dissent from the provinces.

Dissatisfaction with the constitutional deal-making process is widespread, and not only because it has failed to end federal-provincial disharmony. Private, and often secret, discussion and negotiation creates an atmosphere that is not compatible with public affairs in a democracy. When the Prime Minister of Canada described his approach to constitutional negotiation in the Meech round as a question of "rolling the dice," he touched off a controversy over the relationship of citizens to the constitutional reform process that added a new element to the traditional difficulties of reaching constitutional agreement. Canadians may show little patience with constitutional negotiations, but they want more say in the outcome.

This book is designed to inform the reader about what is at stake in the constitutional politics of the nineties. It provides critical analysis and commentary on the issues raised by the September 1991 Mulroney-Clark proposals. Authors examine the substantive questions raised by constitutional reform so that Canadians will be better placed to assess the meaning of constitutional change. In the past governments have sought only the passive assent of citizens to projected reforms, though the Mulroney government has attempted to create more citizen involvement through the Spicer Commission and through the five televised constitutional conferences that were held following the release of the proposals. In any case, a more open and democratic process requires active participation by informed people. This book has the modest aim of assisting citizens in the ongoing public debate on the basic political questions facing Canadians.

The 1991 Mulroney–Clark Proposals

The government's twenty-eight constitutional proposals of September 1991 were divided into three parts. The first part contained seven proposals concerning citizenship rights. It addressed changes to the Charter of Rights and Freedoms that would enshrine property rights and recognize Québec as a distinct society. It proposed a constitutional amendment to recognize the right to aboriginal self-government. It suggested wording for a new "Canada clause" that would add a list of shared values to the constitution. Finally, it proposed a new requirement for provinces seeking to invoke the "notwithstanding clause" that allows provincial legislatures to override provisions of the Charter of Rights and Freedoms for a period of five years. Whereas provincial legislatures now need a simple majority vote (i.e., 50 percent) to do this, the proposal would require a 60 percent majority vote.

The second part contained six proposals concerning federal institutions. Addressing reform of political institutions, it called for an elected, effective and more equitable Senate. Supreme Court appointments would be made from lists submitted by the provinces and territories. The government declined to make a proposal to change the amending formula for the constitution.

Part three contained fifteen proposals that have to do with federal and provincial economic powers. It proposed constitutional amendments to expand the scope of the market economy to include free movement of people, capital and services, as well as goods, and to give the federal government more authority to manage the economy, provided it first secured wide provincial consent (the support of seven provinces with 50 percent of the total population). It would have entrenched executive federalism in the constitution through the creation of a new Council of the Federation. New spending initiatives by the federal government to establish national programmes in areas of provincial jurisdiction were to be subject to wide provincial consent (again, the "seven and 50" rule) and provinces would have gained the constitutional right to opt out of these programmes with financial compensation, if they agreed to establish programmes with comparable objectives.

As well, the proposals would have recognized exclusive provincial jurisdiction in a number of areas, including labour-force training. Most important, the constitution would be amended so that powers could be delegated by one level of government to another with the consent of the legislatures involved. The federal government offered to eliminate the power it now has to declare a "work" or a specific public project in provincial jurisdiction to be in the general interest of Canada and to transfer jurisdiction to the federal government. Moreover, it prepared to turn over to the provinces the residual powers now available to the federal parliament to legislate in non-national areas not identified as either federal or provincial under the existing division of powers.

The government included for discussion issues that do not require constitutional change as such. Prominent among these were procedural reforms to the House of Commons, limiting the role of the Bank of Canada to fighting inflation, and suggestions for harmonizing economic policies between the two levels of government and streamlining government. As well, the government was ready to discuss administrative agreements with the provinces in immigration, cultural programmes and broadcasting. On the important question of Senate reform, the 1991 proposals allowed the joint parliamentary committee to make specific recommendations as to how the elected Senate would be constituted, but it suggested that aboriginal peoples be directly represented, and that Senate votes require a double (French-English) majority. In this fashion a majority of francophone Senators and of anglophone Senators would be required to approve matters of language and culture.

Some sense of the government's priorities can be found in the introduction to the proposals. Here the list of changes begins with the rights of aboriginal peoples. Recognition of Québec as a distinct society comes second, Senate reform is third and economic issues are fourth. While the government had to address its first three priorities through the constitutional reform process, the economic reforms could be made through administrative agreements with the provinces, and in reforming the Bank of Canada and some other matters, the government could act on its own. In parallel to the constitutional process, the government embarked on consultations on a so-called prosperity agenda, which was a way of putting the economic issues on a separate track.

Taken together, the 1991 proposals reveal the political agenda of the government. They offered something to each of the regions and key groups that have supported the government in the past, or that pose a potential threat to its constitutional objectives. The proposal on aboriginal self-government recognized the power of Canada's native peoples to block constitutional reform as they did in the Meech round, acting through Elijah Harper in the Manitoba Legislature. The elected Senate was designed to pre-empt the Reform Party in the West, particularly in the Tory stronghold of Alberta. The distinct society clause attempted to reduce the appeal, in the other Conservative bastion, of the sovereignty option advocated by the Bloc Québécois.

The economic initiatives had the support of the major business lobby groups that not only backed Conservative party policies on free trade, privatization and deregulation, but that played such an important role in getting the Conservatives re-elected in 1988. They reflected a consistent approach to public affairs that the Conservatives have followed since they were first elected in 1984. These initiatives were given such prominence in the constitutional proposals because the proposals were primarily a basis for securing political support. The message was that constitutional reform is a necessary condition for economic prosperity. This is the basis on which the Mulroney government is prepared to seek support for re-election.

Canadians face a dilemma. A Tory government that has lost considerable support and holds little public confidence has been managing constitutional change at a time when there is a real threat to the existence of Canada. Arguably, the crisis over Québec's place in Canada is to some extent a creation of the Mulroney government. But even an early election of a new government would be unlikely to settle the question of Québec's relationship to Canada.

Crisis Politics

During the negotiations to adopt the Meech Lake Accord, political leaders attempted to manipulate public opinion in order to further their own negotiating ends and strengthen their political futures. To assure the passage of the Meech agreement, the Tory government placed great public pressure on dissenting provincial governments. Through the use of staged events and dramatic public appearances surrounding first ministers' meetings, a sense that the failure of what the government called the "Québec round" of negotiations would lead to the break-up of the country was encouraged in all who watched. It was especially encouraged by the media who watched for us. Announcements timed to signal impending success, and to downplay discord, were a constant feature of the debate, so much so that the constitutional issues at stake were overshadowed. The concern became who was going to win the political contest.

When the accord failed in the Manitoba Legislature for reasons which had everything to do with the federal government's unwillingness to take up native people's issues and little to do with its agenda for Québec, the crisis manufactured to secure assent to the accord erupted nonetheless. The Québec government withdrew from further constitutional negotiations and declared its intention to deal in the future only with the federal government. Québec had gone into the Meech round with five minimum demands. This time, following the Bélanger-Campeau and Allaire reports, the Québec government started with the maximum on the table. While Québec blamed public opinion in the rest of Canada for the failure of Meech, the Tories launched a major campaign to discredit Clyde Wells, Jean Chrétien and others. It is hard to escape the conclusion that the manipulators of crisis not only lost control over the situation, they made it worse.

As this round of constitutional politics builds to a head, decisions will be made about what to support or reject, and whom to line up with, and against. Another crisis is to be expected, or more precisely, a series of crises. The major media will assist in the creation of dramatic tension by focusing on the words, actions and gestures of the political players. Like it or not, Canadians are to be the captive audience for the constitutional negotiations. In seeking approval for its constitutional changes, the government has indicated that it may submit the package to the Canadian people for approval in a referendum, or at least in a non-binding plebiscite.

The Shape of a Tory Constitution

The nature of the relationship between various Québec governments and the federal power is the subject of Part I of this book, "The Québec Agenda." In Chapter 1, I situate the roots of the current crisis in the inability of Canada outside Québec to recognize the legitimacy of the constitutional demands set out by Québec over the past thirty years. In Chapter 2, François Rocher accounts for the reaction in Québec to the failure of the Meech Lake Accord by putting it in historical perspective. He points to the need for both a symbolic recognition of

Québec's aspirations and concrete measures that respond to Québec's agenda, notably a constitutional veto and additional powers. Chapter 3 by François Houle assesses the concerns raised outside Québec by the distinct society idea, and considers its chances of finding favour within Québec. Chapter 4 by John D. Whyte looks at issues raised by the Tory decision not to propose changes to the current amending formula for the constitution. In contrast to Rocher's position and my own, Whyte outlines the case for denying Québec a constitutional veto.

Part II of the book, "Constitutional Economics," evaluates the government's economic agenda. Chapter 5 by David Schneiderman analyses the legal constraints that could be placed on governments if the proposals to enlarge the economic-union dimensions of the constitution are accepted. Chapter 6 by Andrew Jackson analyses the impact of an enlarged market clause on the ability of governments to resist the north-south pull on the economy and the country. In Chapter 7, A. W. Johnson looks at devolution of power proposals that could result in weakening both the federal government and the federal system. In Chapter 8, Michael Bradfield assesses the meaning of economic integration for regional economies characterized by high unemployment and disparities of wealth and income. Chapter 9 by George Ross shows how debates within the European Community compare to Canadian federalism. These chapters point out the ideological character of the decision to include economic issues in the constitution. The 1991 proposals would strengthen the wider Conservative agenda of reducing the role of government through adopting free trade, limiting government spending, and narrowing national objectives to inflation fighting and competitiveness.

In Part III, "Strengthening Rights," the authors address new issues raised in the context of changes to the Canadian political culture engendered by the Charter of Rights and Freedoms. The implications of the 1991 proposals are evaluated in Chapter 10 on property rights by Joel Bakan and in Chapter 11 on the rights of native peoples by Radha Jhappan. Chapter 12, by Alexandra Dobrowolsky, examines constitutional change from the perspective of women's equality rights. In Chapter 13, David P. Shugarman looks at what is implied by a charter of social and economic rights, as initially raised by the Ontario government of Bob Rae. Taken together, these contributions underscore the need for constitutional change to embrace an agenda that goes beyond meeting the concerns of Québec.

Part IV, "Constitutional Democracy," presents the wider issues raised by the Mulroney-Clark proposals. In Chapter 14, Miriam Smith looks at reform of the House of Commons and the proposal for an elected Senate from the perspective of whether our federal political institutions are failing us. In Chapter 15, Philip Resnick describes the Western influence on the constitutional agenda with an emphasis on the split between the social democratic and conservative versions of what the West wants. Jane Jenson, in Chapter 16, shows the weaknesses of the current process of constitutional change and suggests how to make this negotiation the "democracy round."

It is in the spirit of promoting understanding of the issues raised by constitutional politics that the essays assembled in this book were prepared. Each chapter has its own introduction by the editors of this volume. As the constitutional drama unfolds, some of the specific proposals discussed in this book will be modified and others will be set aside. But the basic themes of constitutional discussion remain as presented here: Québec, the economy, rights and democracy. Canadians have begun to see themselves less as spectators at constitutional events and more as participants in a political undertaking. These chapters are designed to assist this transformation. They provide not just critical commentary on specific proposals, important as this may be; they also exhort governments to do better, and point the way for citizens to become more aware of the democratic capacity to shape the future.

Part I:
The Québec Agenda

Chapter 1
The Asymmetrical Alternative

Duncan Cameron

The place of Québec in Canada has been at the heart of the constitutional debates for the last thirty years. Unless the traditional concerns of Québec for additional powers and a constitutional veto can be addressed, there seems to be little chance of averting a break-up of Confederation. Duncan Cameron argues that asymmetrical federalism provides a satisfactory way out of the current impasse. A strong central government combined with different status for Québec constitutes less of a threat to the continued existence of Canada than does a refusal to take into account Québec's long-standing constitutional concerns.

In a real sense the national crisis foretold by André Laurendeau and Davidson Dunton in the 1967 report of their Royal Commission on Bilingualism and Biculturalism is now upon us. Dissatisfaction with federalism is widespread in Québec. Even if some constitutional accommodation is reached, the next Québec election is likely to be about sovereignty. For the first time there is a group of Québec members of Parliament, the Bloc Québécois, using the House of Commons to advocate sovereignty for Québec. In the next federal election, they will campaign on the pledge to take Québec out of

Confederation. If they win a considerable majority of Québec seats, this could be seen as a vote for independence. If the Bloc members subsequently withdraw from Parliament that will indeed provoke the result the PQ aims for: no further authority for the Canadian House of Commons over Québec affairs.

The public impatience with constitutional negotiations over the last thirty years is linked to major differences of understanding. For Canadians outside Québec, this is the period when Québec dominated national politics. Except for the short-lived governments of Joe Clark and John Turner, since 1968 Canada has been led by Pierre Trudeau and Brian Mulroney. These two Québec politicians have been supported by strong delegations from their province in the House of Commons. In addition, from the early 1960s, the time of the Quiet Revolution associated with the Québec Liberal government of Jean Lesage, most of the constitutional debate has been generated by issues raised by Québec. From the decisions to facilitate a separate Québec role in pensions and immigration, to the confrontation over the sovereignty-association that culminated in the 1980 referendum, Québec concerns have dominated the national agenda.

For people in Québec, the picture is strikingly different. The reasonable position, advanced by successive Québec governments, that Québec City is the seat of a government with special responsibilities for the preservation of the French language and culture in North America and that this requires some constitutional recognition by Ottawa and the other provinces, has yet to receive recognition, despite years of almost continuous negotiations. No federal government has come to terms with the most basic proposal for change — namely, that Québec be empowered so that the French-speaking

Canadian minority will never see its rights imperilled by the English-speaking majority. The constitutional package of Pierre Trudeau guaranteed individual language rights through the Charter of Rights and Freedoms. Nonetheless, it manifestly failed to address Québec's requests for a veto over future constitutional change and for additional legislative powers to act on behalf of its citizens.

Because of these differing interpretations of recent political events, the prophecy that Laurendeau and Dunton made in the mid-1960s is coming to pass. For Canadians outside Québec, a people much given to understatement, it is hard to give expression to what many now feel: Canada as we know it is on the verge of coming apart. For people in Québec, whose attachment to Canada should not be underestimated, there is great frustration over the inability to recognize in law the simple fact that Québec is different. Outside Québec, many want to see Québec affirm its allegiance to Canada; the phrase "distinct society" suggests for some that Québec is somehow a superior province. These differences in understanding have been especially marked in the latest series of negotiations. Of course, there are voices in this country who would dispute the idea that differences between Québec and the rest of Canada are a result of any misunderstanding. For the one in five Québecers who have favoured outright independence and for those in Canada outside Québec who are prepared to see Québec leave Confederation rather than accommodate its constitutional demands, real and irreconcilable differences are at the heart of the constitutional debate.

In his appearance before the Bélanger-Campeau Commission, Vincent Lemieux, the esteemed political science professor from Laval University, described the situation as "sort of a two act social drama ... Though, in 1980, a majority in Québec said no to the party that proposed a rupture with Canada; in 1990, Canada said no to a party that nevertheless proposed that Québec not break with Canada ... " Canadians now must make up their minds about the place of Québec in Canada. Act three of the drama is at hand.

Constitutional Amendment

There are three ways of amending the Canadian constitution. The standard formula for change requires the approval of the federal parliament and the legislative assemblies of at least seven provinces representing 50 percent of the Canadian population. For a limited number of matters, including a change to the amending formula itself, unanimity is required. And in some matters the federal government can proceed alone. For instance, it can give up (devolve) federal powers to provinces that agree to take them over, or it can renounce powers without specifically handing them over to the provinces. All the specific proposals made by the government in September 1991 avoid recourse to unanimity.

Despite the "seven and 50" formula, any set of proposals that does not have the agreement of Québec is unlikely to go ahead. This, of course, is a judgement based on the current context. The difference between the legal requirement and the political reality is well recognized. The Supreme Court of Canada, in a constitutional reference on the Trudeau constitutional package prior to the eventual 1982 agreement on patriation, said that while there was no legal obligation for provincial support, there was a "convention" that significant change would require substantial consensus. A convention is a constitutional rule that can be identified but not enforced under law. According to the Supreme Court: "Constitutional convention plus constitutional law equals the total constitution of the country."

By now it should be clear that while Canada can change its constitution without the approval of Québec, the price is to create a consitutional crisis. The only logical conclusion is that a constitutional convention exists that support from Québec is required for constitutional change.

The sticking point of the 1991 Mulroney-Clark proposals, then, was that they did not include a veto for Québec. Without this, it is difficult to imagine anyone making a successful case for Canada in a Québec referendum on federalism or even campaigning for a federalist party in a future provincial election campaign. If people outside Québec do not see this point they fail to understand the nature of the current crisis. *Shaping Canada's Future Together,* which contains the Mulroney-Clark proposals, addresses the amending formula question but does not make a proposal out of fear that the unanimity necessary to change the existing formula will be denied.

Other than granting a veto outright to Québec, which would cause as much trouble as not granting one, there are two ways a Québec veto could be worked into the constitution. In the Meech Lake Accord the number of items requiring unanimity was expanded, giving Québec *de facto* a sort of veto while at the same time giving one to every other province. The government indicated in its 1991 proposals that it still favoured this procedure and would proceed this way with support from the provinces. But this approach could end up making the federal government subservient to the whims of the province that decides to be the most obstinate.

The other way is to devise a system of regional vetoes. The Victoria Charter of 1971 suggested a veto for each province with more than 25 percent of the population. In addition, amendments would require the support of two Atlantic provinces and two Western provinces (comprising 50 percent of the population of Western Canada). Recently, the Beaudoin-Edwards Joint Parliamentary Committee called for a return to the Victoria formula. The government did not include this in its 1991 proposals, however, because it "failed to attract the unanimous support which would be required to change the amending formula."

Acceptance of the Victoria formula would be a more significant advance for Québec and for Canada than the distinct society proposal put forward by the government. Québec would feel more secure, and it would be hard to argue that Canada would be weakened as a result. Still, the Mulroney-Clark proposals did provide one method of recognizing the importance attached by successive Québec governments to acquiring additional powers under the constitution. Proposal 25 provides for a constitutional amendment to allow legislative delegation by one level of government to another through the simple assent of both legislatures. If this amendment were approved under the "seven and 50" formula, conceivably the federal government could agree to delegate legislative authority to Québec in various jurisdictions. Formally, it would be obliged to negotiate such devolution of powers to other legislatures — but it may well be that other provinces would be unwilling to ask for as much as Québec, if indeed they asked for anything at all. The key consideration would be whether financial resources would be transferred to the province along with legislative authority. Other items in the proposals indicate some of the areas in which legislative competence could be transferred.

The issue that divides constitutional experts is how to resolve Québec's desire for additional powers with the expressed views of Canadians outside Québec on the need for a strong central government. The obvious response — accord some powers to Québec, but not to the other provinces — meets with two objections. The first is that all provinces should be treated equally under the constitution. This argument, while superficially attractive, assumes that all provinces now receive equal treatment within Canada. This is not the case. Some provinces make equalization payments, others receive transfers; Prince Edward Island is not the size of Ontario, and so what it wants is equitable treatment, not equal treatment. Québec is the only province to ask for what amounts to special constitutional status. It already has programmes of its own; what it requires is constitutional recognition of its right to remain different, through being accorded some additional powers.

The second objection is that the price of developing this asymmetrical federalism would have to be reduced powers for Québec members of the House of Commons. How could they vote in Ottawa on matters that were under provincial control in Québec but not elsewhere? The answer to this is that the House of Commons is a deliberative body of the whole. Members may be sent to Ottawa to represent their constituents, but they are not there to speak only on matters that affect their constituencies alone. Members routinely vote on matters that may concern only distant areas of the country. Why should increased Québec control over immigration, for example, mean that Québec members have less to offer Canadians on this subject than members from other provinces, including those which receive next to no immigrants?

A division of powers more favourable to Québec would not create distinctions among MPs from Québec and those from elsewhere any greater than already exist between the member from a wealthy Toronto suburb and one from an outlying region. The arguments over federalism show that what is needed is a system that is more responsive to the needs of each region, including Québec. The leap of imagination needed to accommodate different economic and social circumstances in the same constitution should be easier to make than the decision to force the majority of Québecers who want renewed federalism to choose the sovereignty option by default.

It should be remembered that many of the powers now sought by Québec were originally in provincial jurisdiction under the 1867 division of powers. It was the use of the spending power by the federal government in areas of provincial jurisdiction that led Québec to reclaim these powers for itself. This same spending power created many of the social programmes that now define modern Canada, including medicare. It should not be impossible to return these powers to Québec alone and permit an asymmetry whereby Canada outside Québec enjoyed the benefits of national programmes.

Chapter 2
Québec's Historical Agenda

François Rocher

Québec looks at all proposals for constitutional change from a historical perspective. The 1991 Mulroney-Clark proposals have to be seen in the context of the debate that has been going on since the 1960s over the division of powers. After the failure of the Meech Lake Accord, both the Québec Liberal Party's Allaire Report and the Québec National Assembly's Bélanger-Campeau Report proposed a major transfer of power to Québec. The Bélanger-Campeau Commission considered the sovereignty option in some detail. In this chapter, François Rocher provides the background for understanding Québec's approach to the 1991 proposals.

The importance of the constitution to various Québec governments over the last three decades can be explained by two complementary factors. On the one hand, since the Quiet Revolution, Québecers have discovered that they are in a position to control the main aspects of their economic, social and political life. On the other hand, they now realize that they must have the political means to exercise this control.

Federalism implies a more or less clear division of powers between the federal and provincial governments.

Moreover, these institutional forms imply a particular vision of Canada. The constitution is not an ordinary legal document. It defines the operational system which prevails in the federation but also conveys a vision of Canada as it is and the place held by each of its components — territorial (the provinces), national (the peoples) and social (the groups and individuals). The constitutional debate is sustained by conflicting visions of the rôle and the place of each level of government in the conduct of public affairs. This is even more the case in Québec, where the "national question" must be taken into account.

In order to understand the evolution of Québec's constitutional position during the past decades, it is important to recall the BNA Act itself. On the one hand, the 1867 constitution explicitly conferred on Québec's French majority, for the first time in its history, "self-government" through the implementation of a certain degree of political autonomy.[1] On the other hand, Confederation was perceived as a "pact" between the provinces. It was the only way to put an end to the political instability that had marked the Union. Only federalism could respond both to the pronounced regionalism of the Maritime provinces and to Lower Canada's aspirations. The BNA Act was interpreted not only as a federation of provinces but also as a federation of nationalities and beliefs. On uniting in a federation, the provinces had no intention of renouncing their autonomy. Thus the preservation of provincial rights became a dominant political theme *vis-à-vis* the federal government.

A New Political Status for Québec?

The 1960s were a turning point with regard to how Québec envisioned its future within the Canadian federation. In 1953 Premier Duplessis appointed a Royal Commission of Enquiry on Constitutional Problems (the Tremblay Commission), whose mandate stressed the need for Québec to preserve provincial prerogatives stemming from the BNA Act in response to Ottawa's avowed intention to proceed with a greater centralization of powers. The election of the Lesage government in 1960 marked a profound change in perception and strategy. Political autonomy was proposed, not as a means of limiting Ottawa's pernicious influence, but as a means of restoring the French-Canadian nation politically, economically and socially. Nationalist thinking thus took a new turn: the necessity of preserving French Canada's traditional character was superseded by the need for national assertion which required defending the powers of the provinces, powers deemed essential to the task of modernization the Québec state had tackled.

It is important to recall that it was Québec's Liberal Party that first insisted on the need for constitutional reform in Canada. At a federal-provincial conference held in July 1960, a few weeks after his election, Premier Jean Lesage invited his colleagues to undertake a readjustment of Canadian federalism. However, the changes demanded mainly dealt with certain federal institutions and did not touch on the division of powers. The Québec government wished to discuss the repatriation of the constitution, the amending formula, the creation of a constitutional court and the adoption of a Charter of Rights. During Lesage's first two years, the watchword was the exercise of Québec's full provincial "sovereignty." Afterwards, the rhetoric was considerably altered.

Lesage came to link Québec's place in the federation with the problem of French-Canadian survival. He called for a review of the division of powers and for an examination of the relations between the two "ethnic groups" which form Canada. This became a central issue in Québec. A large portion of Québec's political class, notably in the Union Nationale, saw that relations between the English and French communities had to be reassessed. Thus, editorialists and intellectuals viewed the establishment of a federal enquiry on the Canadian linguistic and cultural reality as an indispensable step.

During the first half of the 1960s, the constitutional debate centred on the federal proposal to repatriate the constitution and to insert an amending formula known as the Fulton-Favreau solution. Even though Lesage felt that discussions based on this proposal were a preliminary step towards a constitutional revision of the division of powers, opposition members and nationalist forces strongly opposed them. They saw the Fulton-Favreau proposal as a strait-jacket that would make any future extension of Québec's powers impossible (the amendments concerning provincial jurisdictions required unanimity). Also, the proposal conferred on Québec a status identical to that of other provinces (whereas Québec demanded a special status). Lesage felt that the adoption of the formula would entail a substantial political price and was thus forced to reject it. This refusal was fraught with consequences. After Lesage, successive Québec governments would all insist upon the need for concrete results on the division of powers before agreeing to repatriation and an amending formula.

The Laurendeau-Dunton Commission on Bilingualism and Biculturalism had a major impact on the political debate and constitutional negotiations. Its studies underlined the profound nature of the crisis facing Canada and the deterioration of French Canadians' status across Canada and within Québec. The Commission's 1965 *Preliminary Report* insisted upon the need to recognize French Canadians as equal partners in Canada. Should this be denied, the worst possible scenario was forecast.[2] In other words, it warned that the possibility of independence should not be taken lightly.

The commission's analysis made a big impression in Québec, where the idea that Canada was composed of two equal nations was already widespread. Even Lesage became its exponent during a trip in Western Canada. Throughout his journey, he insisted upon the dual aspect of the Canadian problem: on the one hand, Canadian duality required a policy of bilingualism and of equality of rights while on the other hand, the centralizing federal state had to agree to increased powers for Québec — which meant favouring asymmetry. Lesage's comments were met with a somewhat hostile reaction. This only confirmed the difficulty of revising the division of powers.

The election of a Union Nationale government in 1966 provoked a change in tone and perspective. This is best summarized by the slogan adopted by Daniel Johnson's troops: "Equality or Independence." Johnson recalled that as a nation, French Canadians had attempted to identify themselves with a territory and with the provincial state as the only political instrument they could control and use to ensure their development. Thus, Johnson advocated the recognition of two founding nations and arrived at the logical conclusion that the constitution had to be an instrument of equality between the two. He held that the Canadian constitution was particularly inadequate to reconcile the two contradictory approaches which existed in Canada: while the French-Canadian nation demanded more powers for the Québec government, English Canada called for greater political unification. A new constitution was required because the contemporary evolution of federalism had in effect modified its original intent. The new constitution had to recognize Canada's binational character in its political, economic and social structures. Among other things, this meant the adoption of a charter of national (that is, collective) rights concurrently with a charter of human rights.[3] In November 1967, inspired by this approach, Johnson attended the Interprovincial First Ministers' Conference, *The Confederation of Tomorrow.* The issues Johnson raised aroused little interest among his peers, who were more concerned with problems of government co-operation and co-ordination, the transfer of resources and fiscal matters.

Early in 1968, Prime Minister Pearson convened a federal-provincial conference on the constitution, setting in motion the process which led to the Victoria Charter of 1971. However, in the interim, political leadership changed. Prime Minister Pierre Elliott Trudeau, elected in 1968, faced a young, more pragmatic Québec premier, Robert Bourassa, elected in 1970. While the need to review the constitution had initially been requested by Québec in the 1960s, the federal government was now in control of the process of revising the constitution in light of its own objectives. And Ottawa's logic was not the same as Québec's.

Throughout this process of constitutional negotiations, the two-nations thesis had been contested by federal and provincial representatives. However, in contrast to his predecessors, Bourassa attempted less to rewrite the constitution on the basis of the recognition of the two nations than to reform the federal system, securing special status for Québec as well as the resources required for the preservation and development of the Canadian federation's binational character, and especially of Québec's cultural sovereignty. But an increase in Québec's legislative powers was still on the government's mind. From a strategic angle, Bourassa wanted to test English Canada's willingness to alter the division of powers. Adopting a step-by-step approach, Québec tried to use social policy as a test of the possibility of eventually concluding a wider accord dealing with a revision of jurisdictions.

At the end of these talks, the federal and Québec governments agreed in principle to address income support programmes for welfare and health services. There were opposing views as to how an agreement would be implemented. Ottawa felt that administrative and consultative mechanisms would suffice, while Québec believed it was indispensable that its legislative prerogative be entrenched in the constitution.

The Victoria Charter met Québec's requirements only partially. Among its numerous elements were recognition of political and linguistic rights, an amending formula giving Québec a veto over future constitutional amendments and two clauses on the sharing of powers in social policy matters. But the Victoria Charter was devoid of references to the notions of nation, of community or of a Québec people. This was a significant rebuff to Québec. Moreover, on social policy, only the federal government had jurisdiction, although it was required to undertake consultations with the provinces, and it had to comply with their outcome. In Québec, the opposition to the Victoria Charter was harsh and widespread. The document represented a rejection of issues considered to be crucial, such as national recognition and a partial readjustment of powers. Finally, under substantial political pressure, Robert Bourassa was obliged to reject the Victoria Charter in spite of the fact that an endorsement in principle had been given a few days earlier.

It was only in 1975 that constitutional questions once again became a priority. To counter Trudeau's threat to repatriate the constitution unilaterally, Bourassa launched a provincial election in November 1976. During the election campaign, the Québec Liberal Party's constitutional platform reiterated Québec's traditional demands, notably the right of veto, participation in the process of appointing Supreme Court judges, precedence in matters relating to education and culture, the right of opting out of federal programmes with financial compensation, increased powers over immigration and limitations on Ottawa's declaratory and spending powers.[4] Two pledges by the Parti Québécois contributed to its electoral victory in 1976: to act as "a good government" with regard to public administration and, at the constitutional level, to hold a referendum on the question of national sovereignty. Given its commitment, the PQ government had to conduct this referendum before the end of its first mandate.

The Parti Québécois government outlined its position in a White Paper submitted in 1979, entitled *The New Québec-Canada Accord*, which gave a very negative account of the Canadian experience. It held that the francophones had never been considered as a society with a history, a culture and aspirations of their own. Their assimilation had always been the anglophones' main goal. Anglophones had systematically refused to recognize the collective rights of Québec francophones, rights which had to be ensured by the assignment of special powers to Québec's government. According to the PQ, the entire history of federalism, since its inception in 1867, had been tainted by the central government's desire to infringe on areas of provincial jurisdiction.

Four elements explained the centralizing tendencies observed in the Canadian federation according to the PQ. First, centralization corresponded to the aspirations of the English-Canadian community which viewed the central government as an instrument of progress. Second, the central government had taken advantage of times of crisis to invade provincial fields of jurisdiction. Third, the BNA Act furthered the central government's expansion by conferring the residual power on the federal government. Finally, the central government had more financial resources at its disposal than the provinces. The "renewed federalism" proposed by English Canada was merely a set of superficial touch-ups with respect to the central government's role and powers. These reforms would never result in the recognition of the Québec nation or confer a special place for Québec within the federation.

According to the PQ White Paper, a new accord between Québec and the rest of Canada implied the adoption of a new constitutional formula. Such a formula would take into account the concern of Québecers who wished to communicate directly and freely with their neighbours and other nations alike and who did not intend to destroy Canada nor be completely separated from it. Sovereignty-association would be the perfect solution. It would respect Québecers' feelings towards Canada, preserve the economic community, and ensure Québec's autonomy by recognizing powers which the other provinces would not be obligated to claim. Sovereignty-association would establish a more egalitarian relationship between francophones and anglophones, since it would essentially be an association between sovereign states inspired by the proven formula of economic integration.

In order to unite the nationalist forces as much as possible and to ensure victory, PQ strategists opted for a referendum question which incorporated Québecers' traditional demands. Thus, Québecers were asked to give their provincial government a mandate to negotiate a new accord with Canada, based on the recognition of the equality of the two nations. The acceptance of the new status to be negotiated was postponed to a second referendum. The respective Yes and No camps divided mainly on a partisan basis. The Yes camp was mostly identified with the Parti Québécois.

The hopes of provincial government strategists that those who supported an increase in the Québec state's powers would approve of the government's approach were quashed by the strategy adopted by the opposing forces. Even though the question was limited to a possible negotiation "as equals" with Canada, the provincial Liberals, flanked by Ottawa, focused the debate on the independence of Québec.

Québecers were told that if they voted "No" they were opting for a renewal of Canadian federalism that would grant Québec a larger place. Such was, at least, the reasoning of the No camp leader, Claude Ryan, the leader of Québec's Liberal Party. As to Trudeau and his Ottawa Liberals, they were unwilling to commit themselves along these lines; instead, they played on the ambiguity created by political circumstances. In this context, both sides drew from nationalist ideology. It was thus possible to be both a nationalist and a federalist, without fostering an increased centralization of powers in Ottawa.

Following the results of the 1980 referendum, we witnessed a remarkable reinterpretation of the significance of the No victory. Trudeau immediately stated that Québec had chosen Canada. The support for a strong Québec was reduced to the 40 percent who had voted Yes. This ignored the approximately 70 percent of the population who supported a readjustment of the division of powers in Québec's favour.

The Failure of the Referendum

The failure of the referendum had severe consequences. From a symbolic viewpoint, nationalist rhetoric lost some of its credibility. From a political viewpoint, the federal government exploited the referendum's results, discrediting Québec's claims of the past twenty years in order to impose its project to centralize powers. From a social standpoint, the failure of the PQ project resulted in an important demobilization of nationalist forces.

With the initiative in the hands of the federal government, the negotiations leading to the 1982 repatriation of the Canadian constitution took place. The arguments put forward against the federal proposal now met with less support. Repatriation, accompanied by an amending formula and a Charter of Rights, was achieved after intense federal-provincial negotiations. The process resulted in Québec's isolation as the only province which refused to sign the 1982 constitution.

The Charter of Rights, entrenched in the 1982 constitution, attempted to redefine the individual identity of citizens by moulding a new political culture for all Canadians. Canadians would base their allegiance to Canada on the federal institutions that served as guardians of the Charter. But the Charter levels out provincial legislatures and reduces the social differences between them: it is considered by many Québecers as a document that denies their aspirations. The federal *coup de force* raised few protests in English Canada. Of course, the Québec National Assembly condemned Ottawa's action with a unanimous vote of all parties, but without rousing passions in Québec.

It was two years before discussions resumed between Ottawa and Québec at the initiative of the Mulroney government. In response to the Conservative electoral promise to bring Québec back into the Canadian constitutional family with "honour and enthusiasm," Premier Lévesque decided that it was worth taking the "beautiful risk." In May 1985, he submitted to the Mulroney government twenty-two conditions for having Québec's signature on the Canadian constitution. As a whole, this document once again set out Québec's traditional demands for the right of veto, an increase in provincial powers (communications, immigration, international relations, and so on), the restriction of the application of the Charter of Rights to articles pertaining to democratic rights and, finally, the constitutional recognition of Québec as a distinct society. However, because of the upcoming provincial elections, the Mulroney government was not eager to undertake negotiations with the PQ government.

The election of Robert Bourassa's Liberal government in 1985 considerably modified the Québec political climate and the tone of federal-provincial negotiations. A minimalist and gradual approach was adopted. The proposals were — and were intended to appear — reasonable, considering the tumultuous history of constitutional negotiations. They represented, for instance, less than Bourassa's previous demands of the 1970–76 period. The Québec government submitted five conditions for its agreement to the 1982 constitution: recognition of Québec's particular character, the right of veto on all future constitutional amendments, limitation of the federal spending power, powers related to immigration matters and participation in the appointment of Supreme Court judges from Québec. The reinstatement of Québec in the Canadian constitutional order was presented as a prerequisite for any discussion of constitutional questions which concern other provinces. Québec decided to defer to a later date the other subjects it intended to negotiate.

The failure of the Meech Lake Accord which embodied these five conditions, however, profoundly changed the terms of the constitutional debate. In Québec, the failure was largely interpreted as a refusal of Québec's demands. It can be explained, among other things, by a failure to understand the "minimalist" strategy adopted by the government of Québec. While the five conditions presented were the strict minimum that Québec could accept, several participants wanted to divide the accord to get only those clauses not requiring unanimity adopted. Bourassa's refusal to go that route made him appear intransigent. Moreover, the discussions surrounding Meech soon brought to light other dissatisfactions.

Several provinces and social groups, including native peoples, wanted to use the opportunity to press their constitutional demands. It became impossible to satisfy Québec's demands without taking into account the constitutional amendments sought by other provinces and social groups as a whole. Finally, the failure of Meech provided the opportunity to grasp fully the magnitude of the conflict between the Canadian and Québec visions of Canada. Although only two provinces (representing 7 percent of the Canadian population) refused to sign the agreement, the polls demonstrated that a substantial majority of Canadians (between 60 and 70 percent) were opposed to the Meech Lake Accord.[5] It therefore came up against two contradictory visions of Canada, pitting the principle of the equality of the provinces against the principle of asymmetry — special powers for Québec.

Chapter 3
The Distinct Society Clause
François Houle

Words and the use of language are an important part of constitutional negotiations. The phrase distinct society, *used to describe Québec in the Meech Lake Accord, became a focus of controversy. For some, it signalled approval for Québec's longstanding position that it needs more powers to ensure its survival as a francophone society within Canada. For others, it was a purely symbolic recognition that Québec was different. In this chapter, François Houle shows the centrality of a distinct society clause to the success of constitutional reform.*

With the notion of *distinct society,* the federal government proposes to recognize in the Canadian constitution Québec's specific characteristic as the primary homeland of francophones in Canada. The government has judged that, without the formal recognition of that reality, it is not likely that the majority of francophone Québecers will accept the constitutional proposals and thereby adhere to the 1982 Canadian constitution. Indeed, the absence of such a clause is bound to lead, in the short term, to a deterioration of the political debate and even to the independence of Québec and the dismemberment of Canada as we know it.

For a large number of francophone Québecers, acceptance of the distinct society clause has come to represent not only recognition of the specific characteristics of their society, but also an expression or symbol of goodwill on the part of English Canadians of their desire to keep Québec within the Canadian federation. On the other hand, for many English Canadians and for native peoples, the clause appears to negate the existence of other distinct groups in Canada and to lead to the recognition of special status for Québec. Such a position, if it is firmly maintained at all costs, renders the signing of any constitutional agreement virtually impossible. Canada's survival must be put ahead of operational principles such as the absolute equality of the provinces or the uniformity of the services offered to Canadians, if constitutional reform is to succeed.

To ensure the unity of Canada and to put an end to the current round of constitutional negotiations, acceptance of the distinct society clause, regardless of its exact content, appears unavoidable. However, the contents of the clause must be at least minimally acceptable to the majority of Québecers. Moreover, the Canadian constitution will have to reconcile the different visions of Canada that result from the existence of different national identities and must not attempt to impose the vision of the dominant group.

The notion of distinct society seems to many Canadians to have emerged with the Meech Lake Accord in 1987, yet that was only a new formulation of Québec's chief request dating back to the first half of the 1960s. Québec had long linked its acceptance of a constitutional amending formula to a new division of powers. Successive Québec governments aimed at a clearer definition of Québec's powers and at an enhancement of those powers. Thus, Québec demanded more powers in cultural and linguistic matters (Lesage, 1964–66), in social policy matters (Johnson and Bertrand, 1966–70), and again in culture and social policy (this was why Bourassa rejected the Victoria Charter).

In fact, if the successive governments of Québec attempted to use the negotiations on the amending formula to force a new distribution of powers, it was because Québec was convinced that its francophone character had to be protected. To do so, Québec maintained that it needed new powers, or at least more autonomy, in exercising the ones it already had. Fuelled by the work of the Royal Commission on Bilingualism and Biculturalism and the upheavals of the Quiet Revolution, francophone Québecers became increasingly aware of the need to protect their distinctive characteristics and to control certain mechanisms of power. This was first evidenced in Québec's demands for greater autonomy in the areas of culture and language. Then, greater control over social policies appeared necessary to maintain that specificity, and finally, new powers over immigration became, in the mid-1970s, a major request of Québec governments.

These various formulations of the requests of the successive Québec governments took on different names over the years: special status, asymmetrical federalism, distinct society. But the underlying objective was always the same. It always involved granting Québec the powers needed — or at the very least setting up a system that would enable it to acquire them — so that Québec could preserve its society within Canada.

It is no wonder, then, that the government of Québec could not bring itself to sign the 1982 constitutional accord, which afforded satisfaction neither on the amending formula nor on a new division of powers that would have allowed Québec to achieve special status. It would be wrong to conclude, however, that the failure of the constitutional talks during the 1960s and 1970s is attributable to the fact that the provinces of English Canada wanted Québec to be treated in the same way as all the other provinces. In fact, during that era, Québec was able to set up its own pension plan independent of the existing federal pension plan, and the federal government reached an agreement with the Lévesque government granting it greater powers in matters of immigration (the Cullen-Couture agreement).

That different relations existed between Québec and the federal government than between the other provinces and the federal government in certain areas (the pension plan, immigration and international relations, especially with the francophone countries) did not represent a threat to Canada. Experience seems to demonstrate that even when powers are not identical for all provinces, this does not mean that some Canadians are second-class citizens. The constitutional issues discussed during the twenty-five years preceding the Meech Lake Accord indicate that what is difficult for English Canadians to accept today — namely, recognizing Québec as a distinct society — has not previously posed insuperable problems.

The Québec Liberal Party took those constitutional dynamics into account when it proposed, in its 1985 document entitled *Maîtriser l'avenir* (*Controlling Our Future*), five points which, if satisfied, would enable Québec to reintegrate into the Canadian constitution. Understandably, the demand that Québec be explicitly recognized as a distinct society and be granted a constitutional veto are among the five points. That position did not arouse opposition when tabled, and some even commented that the demands were minimal compared to Québec's traditional request to begin by establishing a new division of powers. In 1986, the provincial premiers agreed to resume the constitutional talks on the basis of Québec's demands, and they met with Prime Minister Mulroney at Meech Lake on April 30, 1987. The resulting agreement was to divide Canada and to give rise to one of the most bitter constitutional debates ever.

In the Meech Lake Accord, which was initially accepted in 1987 by all the provinces, the recognition of Québec's specific needs is found in an interpretive rule that states: "The constitution of Canada shall be interpreted in a manner consistent with … the recognition that Québec constitutes within Canada a distinct society." In addition, it states that it is "the role of the legislature and Government of Québec to preserve and promote the distinct identity of Québec." Because the provinces and the federal government were unable to come to an agreement on a new division of powers, it was left to the courts to define those powers on a case-by-case basis.

There are a number of reasons why the concept of distinct society has found such scant support among Canadians outside Québec, though officially, only two provinces (Manitoba and Newfoundland) did not ultimately ratify the Meech Lake Accord. Three criticisms seem particularly significant in explaining the mobilization of forces opposed to the notion of distinct society. First, many Canadians seemed to find it difficult to accept the fact that the Meech Lake Accord made room in the constitution of Canada for a vision of Canada espoused by Québec but not for the visions of native peoples or English Canadians. Second, the notion of distinct society might, according to some, enable Québec to exert certain legislative powers that the other provinces would not have; this roused the defenders of the new dogma of provincial equality, such as Newfoundland Premier Clyde Wells. Third, the fact that the distinct society clause would allow the government of Québec to bypass the Canadian Charter of Rights and Freedoms without having to resort to the "notwithstanding clause" seemed to some to be a denial of the equality of Canadian citizens.

Further, some in English Canada expressed concern that the distinct society clause could be used by the government of Québec to undermine or threaten other equality rights in the name of protecting Québec's distinct society. For example, they asked, could the government of Québec use the distinct society clause to justify government policies that discriminated against women or restricted the rights of ethnic or religious minorities? Did the equality rights set out in the Charter override the distinct society clause, or did the distinct society clause override equality rights?

The 1991 federal proposals took up the distinct society clause again but, to quell criticism, its scope was reduced considerably compared to the wording in the Meech Lake Accord. The distinct society clause was now to appear in the Charter itself, as one of a series of statements that confer rights on individuals as members of communities. These collective rights — the rights of women, the rights of ethnic minorities, and the rights of aboriginal peoples — are already assured in four sections of the Charter. Equality of the sexes and multiculturalism are restated in sections 27 and 28 of the Charter because of the fact that legislatures can override section 15 (where they first appear). The distinct society clause would now be simply a part of this restatement, appearing as a new subsection to section 25. There is nothing in the clause or in the Charter to suggest that the distinct society clause takes precedence over any other rights. In addition, the distinct society clause would be subject to the general section 1 limitation that applies to all other rights granted in the Charter, that is, that all the enumerated rights are subject to such "reasonable limits" as can be "demonstrably justified in a free and democratic society." This reading of the clause is shared by equality-seeking groups, such as the National Action Committee on the Status of Women, which is no longer opposed to the distinct society clause.

Furthermore, the distinct society clause in its proposed form specifically mentions the preservation of official-language minorities throughout Canada. Obviously, this includes the preservation of the francophone minority outside of Québec as well as the preservation of the anglophone minority in Québec. And, by defining the term *distinct society* to mean Québec's language, culture and civil law, the interpretative scope of the clause is limited; in contrast, in the Meech Accord the scope of the clause was undefined. Because of the definition of — and thus limitation on — the distinct society clause, this issue may become a central theme in the constitutional debate in Québec. Lise Bissonnette has already described the definition in the federal proposals as a "folkloric" definition of Québec's distinctiveness.

It is important to note that by proposing to place the distinct society clause in the Charter, the federal government has ensured that no new powers are conferred on the government of Québec. The government of Québec is not mentioned in the clause itself. The Charter specifically states (section 31) that none of its provisions extends the powers of legislatures (including the Québec National Assembly). The clause cannot be used to increase the authority or powers of the Québec National Assembly. While this may be welcomed in the rest of Canada, it will not be welcomed in Québec, where a revision of the division of powers has been a main objective for almost thirty years.

The reduction in the scope and meaning of the notion of distinct society enables us to understand why there has been less opposition to the notion from the political leaders in English Canada. Clyde Wells, adversary *par excellence* of the notion of distinct society contained in the Meech Lake agreement, finds the 1991 federal proposals on this point acceptable. The notion of distinct society is also acceptable to Michael Harcourt of British Columbia, "as long as it does not imply different powers for Québec." Manitoba's constitutional committee in its report says that it prefers the term *unique* to *distinct,* but that in any event, Québec "should not have special powers." It would seem that a number of people prefer the new definition of distinct society since it is largely symbolic and has little chance of allowing the government of Québec to exercise any new powers or to broaden the scope of its existing powers. It is unfortunate that some politicians in English Canada are willing to accept more readily that Québec weigh collective rights against individual rights than to accept that Québec exercise certain special powers.

Clearly, the proposed wording of the distinct society clause meets the historic demands of Québec to a very minimal degree, at best. Consequently, it is altogether possible that this wording will be unacceptable to the majority of francophone Québecers who wish to remain in Canada, since it only protects what has already been gained in language, culture and civil law, and has no chance of ever affecting the division of powers. It is therefore important that those outside Québec not reject from the outset any negotiations that would strengthen the distinct society clause. Although the clause as stated in the September 1991 proposals only recognizes Québec's distinct character, it could, if defined in a broader sense, allow Québec to achieve a greater margin of autonomy without taking anything away from the rest of Canada.

The concept of distinct society has the potential to incorporate the vision of Canada as perceived by the majority of francophone Québecers. However, the vision of Canada proposed by the native peoples must not be neglected, either. Increasingly, that vision hinges on self-government and the recognition of inherent rights. While one can envision a constitutional reform that incorporates both these visions of Canada, it would be irreconcilable with any vision of Canada that sets forth a federal régime centralized in economic and social terms while at the same time forcefully maintaining the absolute equality of the provinces and the requirement that all Canadians benefit from the same services. If people continue to insist that everything obtained by Québec or everything obtained by the native peoples must also be obtained by the other provinces, it will only lead to dismal failure.

The citizens of English Canada and many provincial governments want a central government capable of providing uniform policies and greater leadership. In contrast, the francophone citizens of Québec, or at least a majority of them, want greater powers for their provincial government. As for the native peoples, it is becoming increasingly clear that they are seeking political institutions of their own, and land, which will allow them to preserve their ancestral values and customs as well as the right to be the architects of their own development.

The current constitutional debate enables us to see very clearly the fragmentation of the national identity, which puts insurmountable limitations on any centralized vision of Canada. Imposing a particular image of

Canada by way of constitutional reform may well lead to the destruction of Canada itself. In the current context, only a constitution defining an asymmetrical federalism has any chance of offering a synthesis of the various visions of Canada and of allowing every group to participate in the definition of the collective destiny it chooses.

Chapter 4
Amending the Constitution

John D. Whyte

The constitution of 1867 did not include a formula for its amendment in Canada. Until the Constitution Act, 1982, changes to Canada's constitution required recourse to Britain. Although the amending formula adopted in 1982 remains controversial, in its 1991 proposals the federal government declined to propose changes. Québec has historically claimed a veto over constitutional change. This was denied in 1982, but it remains on the table. In this chapter, John D. Whyte questions whether the lack of a Québec veto in the 1991 Mulroney-Clark proposals was a fatal omission. He argues that, while there are important grounds for supporting a Québec veto, the amending formula itself is difficult to alter in part because of Québec's own positions in previous constitutional negotiations. Moreover, it is hardly possible to expect the needed unanimity among the provinces and the federal government on changes to the formula.

"This is Canada's round." This bold declaration concludes the Introduction to the federal government's September 1991 constitutional proposals, *Shaping Canada's Future Together*. Indeed, these proposals go far beyond the concerns addressed in the 1987 Meech Lake Accord, which was generally regarded as an instrument of the Québec round. The 1991 proposals treat aboriginal rights, economic integration, alteration of the Senate's role and structure, property rights and economic integration, none of which responds to Québec's traditional concerns and none of which is reflected in Québec's more streamlined agenda for constitutional change announced in May 1986 by Gil Rémillard, the Québec minister responsible for intergovernmental affairs.

A dominant emphasis of the 1991 proposals was, however, renewed (and devolutionary) federalism — either the direct transfer of powers to provincial governments or the facilitation of further provincial legislative jurisdictions. In the same vein the government repeated a version of one of Meech Lake's centrepieces — the reining in of Parliament's spending power in response to its historic use as a device for imposing substantive federal regulatory policy in areas of provincial jurisdiction.

Another major feature of the 1991 proposals was a revised (and, in one reading, strengthened) version of the distinct society clause under which Québec would escape some of the restraining force of the Charter of Rights on cultural and linguistic policy making.

In short, the proposals did not represent an abandonment of the Québec round. Nor should they have. The 1867 Constitution Act could well be inadequate at accommodating the autonomy claims of distinct cultural communities within the federation. After all, the need for constitutional revisions that confer political authority on peoples that feel trapped inside inappropriate political arrangements is not unique to Canada. Finding ways to accommodate liberation politics without breaking existing nations is one of the pervasive challenges of our age. The general nature of this liberating project and, in Canada, the historically central position in constitutional debate of Québec's needs for greater autonomy and the growing recognition of the justice of aboriginal self-government are all factors that underscore the extent to which we must not be beguiled by the rhetoric of a "Canada round." Instead, we must maintain our focus on the chief constitutional issue facing Canada — the development of proposals that recognize immense cultural differences and, at the same time, maintain the integrity of needed national political processes.

The Amending Formula

At the heart of a nation's legal core are the rules that allow national redefinition. The sovereignty concept, by itself, does not disclose where power lies within a nation to express that sovereignty. The foundational authority for the expression of national sovereignty is found in rules for amending the constitution. (That is, of course, except in those cases in which foundational authority is found in extra-legal or revolutionary expressions of popular will or, as is sadly the case in many nations, extraordinary expressions of military and élitist power.)

In Canada, sovereignty in constitutional change is found in the 1982 amending formula which requires that most alterations to the constitution have the consent of the Parliament of Canada and seven provincial legislatures representing provinces whose total population exceeds 50 percent of the population of Canada. Thus, the formula for approving constitutional change does not require the participation of any particular province and, notably, does not require consent from Canada's ethnically distinct peoples — neither aboriginals nor French-speaking Canadians.

This means that Québec as representative of a distinct minority cannot, by itself, forestall constitutional change. Of course, after the creation of the 1982 constitutional amending formula, Québec, like all other provinces, is able to avoid any derogation of its legislative powers through exercising its right to opt out of amendments that impair provincial authority. In this sense, the constitutional arrangements that grant political authority to Québec, and to its predominantly French-speaking population, are not subject to alteration by a national majority.

Nevertheless, Québec has traditionally asked for a veto over constitutional amendments and, in 1986, it reiterated this position as one of its five conditions for reconciliation with the rest of Canada. In the government's 1991 constitutional proposals, the problem is mentioned; however, it is pointed out that changes to the amending formula (including, one assumes, either expanding the matters which require unanimous consent of Parliament and all the provinces, or changing the formula to give Québec a specific veto power) would themselves require unanimous approval. The federal government supports constitutional recognition of a Québec veto but recognizes that unanimity is not probable. However, if complete consensus for an amending formula were to emerge, the federal government would happily accept it.

In any event, Québec's ability to block constitutional amendments continues to depend on finding other provincial allies and, in this way, its power over constitutional change is attenuated. Two questions emerge from this situation. Is a veto power for Québec a logical constitutional expression of Québec's unique position within Canada, as is argued elsewhere in this volume? Second, should the failure to satisfy Québec's condition that a veto power be recognized cause it to reject the current process of constitutional accommodation?

Those who hold that a Québec veto is an essential structural expression of Québec's position in Canada base their position on the metaphor of compact. If Canada had been formed by the agreement of English Canada and French Canada to join together to create a strong nation, one would expect the terms of the federation to be altered only on the consent of both founding nations. If, on the other hand, Canada were a manifestation of imperial policy for the British territories of North America (and federalism was chosen simply because it best reflected the presence of existing and diverse political communities), Québec's claim for a veto could not be derived from Canada's structural origins. The historical truth is neither of these. Confederation was both a domestic initiative and an imperial policy. The case for federalism was not merely a response to the presence of existing communities, it carried forward the special arrangements guaranteed to the French society in North America since the mid-eighteenth century.

Let us leave aside competing accounts of our origins as a country. Canada is now a distinct political entity. Like all other nations it must have the capacity for constitutional reformation when its people consent. A solid, rule-of-thumb approach to national consent in federal states is that at least a majority of the people representing at least a majority of the states or provinces must agree to proposed changes. On the other hand, what does not seem to be an intuitively compelling element of consent is the capacity of one province or state to forestall change for the whole nation. A political unit's capacity to impose external effects far beyond its political accountability makes the widespread adoption of constitutional vetoes highly suspect. The resentment expressed over Newfoundland's failure to adopt the Meech Lake Accord reveals how problematic vetoes are in the process of national constitutional reform.

As long as the particular set of political arrangements under which Québec operates cannot be eroded by national majorities that exclude Québec and the Québec people, which is the case under the 1982 constitution, it may be both unnecessary and unwieldy to place all constitutional reform in thrall to Québec's approval.

It is precisely these ideas of statecraft that to my mind inform the two Supreme Court of Canada decisions dealing with Canada's implicit amendment rules prior to the enactment of the 1982 constitution. In one case the Court upheld the view that the federal principle should be reflected in the measurement of national consent, but in the other case (the Québec Veto case) the Court, having concluded that the federal principle was satisfied, rejected the idea that a single political unit could avert constitutional change. To have held otherwise would have undercut a democratically approved programme of national self-determination.

The third analytic approach is to ask if there is some special condition of Québec (not necessarily rooted in history) that makes its consent a vital condition of legitimate constitutional change. This may be the most compelling case for a Québec veto. Québec represents one-half of Canada's language duality and, in this role, it should have a say in changes to the structure of political authority. The argument against this position is that Québec's authority with respect to matters touching on language and culture is not at stake in most constitutional revision and, if it is, Québec's authority can be protected through the exercise of its rights under the 1982 constitution and under the distinct society clause.

This claim, however, may rest on an overly narrow conception of culture, or on an inflated sense of the range of protection afforded by opting-out provisions or the distinct society clause. One cannot easily dismiss the argument for a veto based on Québec's unique role as the political representative of one of Canada's peoples.

The second question is whether the failure to recognize a constitutional veto for Québec should lead to a rejection by Québec of the process that began in 1991. The historical argument against its rejection by Québec on the grounds of the veto is, of course, that in 1981 the Québec premier endorsed the amending formula that came into force in 1982 and which does not give Québec a veto. Under this view, Québec is regarded as having subscribed to the three essential conditions that amendment rules in the Canadian federation must satisfy. They are that all provinces are to have equal status, that amending the constitution should not be easy but should be possible and that provinces must have their vital interests (and property) protected against the rest of the nation. All of these elements were satisfied in the 1982 constitution with its consent formula and its opting-out provisions.

However, it simply may not be fair to use this historical argument against Québec's claim for a veto. It was a position taken for the very particular purpose of solidifying a coalition of opposition to the federal plan for unilaterally patriating the constitution. It may not seem attractive for a province to participate in exercises of constitutional reform for reasons other than achieving reform, but when the ulterior purposes for participation are known (and, apparently, accepted by the other provinces that participated in devising this particular plan), the pretence of believing that the position taken was a genuine substantive preference would seem to be precluded.

There is a much stronger reason for asking Québec to accept the failure to gain a veto over constitutional amendment. It is this: changes to the amending formula are simply not available because, except in the most extraordinary circumstances, unanimous approval is not available. On this matter, it is fair to hold Québec responsible, in part, for Canada's too-rigid amending formula. The idea of a constitutional veto (with its inevitable capacity for provinces to avoid accountability for the considerable external effects it produces) is an idea traditionally and genuinely supported by Québec. The current barrier to national self-development is analogous to Québec's actual possession of a constitutional veto, an arrangement Québec wanted and, evidently, still wants.

Legislative Delegation and the Amending Formula

There is one final matter with respect to the amending rules. One of the most significant elements of the federal proposals, at least in terms of the possibilities for Québec to develop a stronger political community, is the recommendation that there be "a constitutional amendment which would permit federal and provincial governments to delegate to each other the authority to legislate in a given field." Apart from the question of the desirability of different legislative authorities in different provinces (and the potential consequences for the structure of Parliament), the question arises whether such a constitutional amendment would amount to a change to the amending formula and would thus require the unanimous approval of Parliament and all the provinces. The argument that unanimity is required is based on the claim that the power of delegation is a new method of changing the constitution and thereby is an alteration of the rules for making amendments.

The counter-argument is that section 43 of the Constitution Act, 1982 already explicitly permits bilateral constitutional amendments, which is what such legislative delegations would be. However, because of the somewhat convoluted wording of section 43, it is not at all clear that agreements to delegate legislative authority would fall within the scope of that section. As the document containing the 1991 federal proposals states, legislative delegation was proposed earlier in 1991 by the Beaudoin-Edwards Joint Parliamentary Committee on the Process for Amending the Constitution of Canada. However, the same federal document fails to mention that the Beaudoin-Edwards Committee was also quite clear in suggesting that any changes to the arrangement of legislative powers cannot be constitutionalized through use of section 43's bilateral amendment formula. It would seem, therefore, that a highly important element of the Mulroney-Clark proposals amounts to a change to the amending rules; this proposal could well flounder on the need to obtain the unanimous consent of Parliament and the provinces. The costs of a rigid, veto-based amending formula (a structure that was to be extended in the Meech Lake Accord) will, it seems, create a significant barrier to achieving this important element of the Québec agenda.

We have no choice, then, but to ask Québec to accept the limitations of our current constitutional structure and to see the current attempts as a good-faith effort to achieve those elements of its constitutional reform agenda that are possible. Whether Québec will recognize the unavoidability of only imperfectly realizing its goals remains to be seen.

Part II: Constitutional Economics

Chapter 5

The Market and the Constitution

David Schneiderman

Constitutions normally lay out general principles that have wide acceptance. Yet the 1991 proposals moved towards enshrining a particular economic ideology. In effect, the federal government called for the principles of free market economics to be embedded in the constitution through an amendment that would guarantee the mobility of capital, labour and services, as well as goods, within Canada.

David Schneiderman argues that such a measure could lead governments to restrict the scope of democratic action for fear of distorting market forces. He shows that the Australian example gives Canadians good cause to resist the "constitutionalizing" of a particular economic vision. He questions the wisdom of moving quickly to make such a major change to the constitutional framework of Canada.

Writing in 1947, Bora Laskin, former Chief Justice of Canada, wrote that the Canadian constitution did not "enshrine any particular economic theory." That observation may have been of dubious accuracy then: it would certainly no longer be true if the recent constitutional proposals tabled by the federal government regarding the Canadian common market are entrenched in the constitution.[1] While the proposed guarantee to entrench a Charter right to property has attracted much attention, the common market proposal may be able to do much of the work of a right-to-property clause and much more.

The common market clause would guarantee the free movement of persons, goods, services and capital across provincial and territorial boundaries. Any laws or practices, whether federal or provincial, which act as a restriction or barrier on that mobility would be of no force or effect. The common market principle would not be absolute. Exceptions would be federal laws regarding equalization or regional development, provincial laws which promote regional development within the province but do not treat other regions in the province any more favourably than other provinces, and those federal or provincial laws which are declared to be in the "national interest" by Parliament and receive the approval of the governments of at least seven provinces representing more than 50 percent of the Canadian population (the "seven and 50" rule). Dissenting provinces may not otherwise opt out of the operation of the common market.

A companion proposal would grant the federal government a broad power to legislate "in relation to any matter that it declares to be for the efficient functioning of the economic union." Such laws will also require the approval of the governments of at least seven provinces with more than 50 percent of the population. Dissenting provinces may opt out of the operation of the federal law for a non-renewable three-year period. Neither the declaration of laws in the "national interest" nor the passage of laws "for the efficient functioning of the economic union" may be easily accomplished; the "seven and 50" rule would apply here, too, the same condition that must be met to amend most parts of the constitution.

Free Markets

The common market proposal was offered as a means to correct, and make more efficient, the operation of the free market system. It is argued that, in the era of globalization, Canadian business must be prepared to compete nationally in order to meet the demands of international competition. By targeting government practices which artificially prop up certain enterprises, the proposal will ensure that weak businesses will give way before large, powerful ones; economies of scale will result which, in turn, will permit the Canadian economy to compete more effectively in the international marketplace. Practices such as provincial government procurement policies which favour in-province goods, services and labour have been targeted by the drafters of the proposals.[2] Preferential beer and wine pricing by provincial liquor boards has also been identified as a culprit in limiting interprovincial mobility of alcoholic goods. Marketing boards which set quotas on the production of agricultural goods, and provide farmers with a set price and the right to supply a specific share of the market, also are likely to be caught by the proposed amendment.

These consequences alone are quite significant. But the language of the common market proposals is not limited to such matters and potentially could have much wider implications for the provincial and federal regulation of the marketplace. Economists have identified a number of "distortions" of the marketplace that act as barriers to the free flow of capital and labour, goods and services.[3] Those distortions include provincial government pools of capital, such as the Alberta Heritage Trust Fund and Québec's Caisse de dépôt et placement, which have made available to local enterprises favourable financing at below-market rates.[4] Some provinces impose restrictions on investment by insurance companies, such as restricting investment in real estate, in part, to property within the province.[5] The proposed common market generally would not permit such preferential investment at the local level. Natural resource policies in some provinces are designed to ensure that processing of the resource occurs within the province;[6] some set up regulatory régimes to ensure that the resource needs of the province are met before export is allowed.[7] Provinces which choose to limit resource processing and exports are likely to be offending the principle of the economic union.

A wide variety of less obvious barriers to trade may also be caught.[8] Corporate tax rates may vary from province to province, as do labour standards, and that variation can distort the free flow of capital.[9] Provinces which choose to impose greater corporate tax rates[10] or enforce labour standards such as pay equity, which may increase the costs of doing business in the province and thereby distort the allocation of resources, could be seen to be raising barriers or restrictions to the free movement of capital in the common market. Packaging standards may vary, and rogue provinces which require differing and more onerous standards, such as the requirement of French-language packaging in Québec, may have set up a restriction on the free movement of goods that could be challenged in the courts.[11] Environmental standards also may act as a barrier or restriction.[12] The province of Alberta has, in practice, refused admission into the province of hazardous wastes from Ontario or Québec which may have been destined for disposal at the Swan

Hills waste facility. This practice, which restricts the free passage of hazardous goods into the province of Alberta, may not survive the constitutionalizing of the common market.[13]

Free Trade or Free Enterprise?

It may seem curious that the federal government has proposed constitutional amendments to guarantee the common market when there are a number of other large, and more pressing, matters on the constitutional agenda, such as accommodating Québec's distinctness, aboriginal self-government, and Senate reform. And, as the 1980 federal Liberal government discussion paper, *Securing the Canadian Economic Union,* acknowledged, although some barriers to interprovincial trade exist, Canada has attained a "highly integrated economic union nonetheless."[14] The proposal is even more curious when we are advised, according to most economic estimates, that the cost of these barriers and restrictions to the Canadian public is quite modest (less than 1 percent) when compared to Canada's gross domestic product.[15] But the proposal has a distinguished pedigree, which can be traced back to section 121 of the Constitution Act, 1867, which guarantees that "all articles of the Growth, Produce, or Manufacture of any one of the Provinces shall from and after the Union, be admitted free into each of the other provinces." The section has rarely been the subject of litigation and, as a consequence, judicial treatment. The section has been limited to catching only those fiscal measures which act as barriers between provinces, leaving untouched any measures which regulate the marketplace within the provinces.[16] It was because of the limited effect given to section 121 that, in 1978, the Canadian Bar Association recommended constitutional amendments to this section to guarantee the free mobility of goods, services, labour and capital, which would enable any interested citizen to attack in court any barriers to that movement.[17] This same proposal was made in the 1979 Pepin-Robarts Report,[18] the 1980 Liberal Party of Québec Beige Paper,[19] and the 1980 federal Liberal document *Powers over the Economy,* tabled by then Justice Minister Jean Chrétien.[20] The Macdonald Commission, the intellectual springboard for the Canada-U.S. free trade agreement, also recommended the removal of interprovincial trade barriers, both by strengthening section 121 and by instituting a code of economic conduct to cover those practices which an amended section 121 might not reach.[21]

The call for an unimpeded common market was renewed, more significantly, in the Québec Liberal Party's Allaire Report.[22] The report declared Canadian federalism an economic failure and called for the radical decentralization of federal power together with a common market with the rest of Canada. In briefs and testimony before the Bélanger-Campeau Commission on the Political and Constitutional Future of Québec, the Québec business community, speaking through the Chambre de commerce du Québec, called for the rejection of any restrictions on the "free movement of individuals, goods and capital" throughout Canada.[23] There were no calls for a new corresponding economic power for the federal government.

There also has been some political movement in this direction in recent years. Both the Western and the Maritime premiers have agreed in principle to abandon preferential procurement policies which discriminate against out-of-province businesses within their respective regions. In August 1991, all of the provincial premiers agreed to end preferential procurement policies for goods in excess of $25 000.[24] With the apparently anomalous situation of a free trade agreement in place with the United States and no equivalent agreement amongst the provinces, and with the international pressures at global trade talks to remove certain barriers to trade, the time may have appeared opportune to constitutionalize the market model.[25]

Yet, throughout this debate, not enough attention has been given to the Australian experience of almost ninety years with a similar common market clause.[26] The Australian constitution guarantees in section 92 that "customs, trade, commerce, and intercourse among the states ... shall be absolutely free." The clause, according to law professor Peter Hanks, has "posed a serious obstacle to any government which undertook to regulate commercial activity in Australia."[27] Courts have been faced with the perplexing task of reconciling this free market clause with public demands for state intervention and regulation.[28] The Australian Advisory Committee on Trade and National Economic Management, in its report to the Constitutional Commission, described the impact of section 92 jurisprudence in this way:

> Interstate trade is almost entirely free from taxation, banks and airlines cannot be nationalised, interstate transport cannot be made subject to discretionary licensing, and most marketing schemes must exempt interstate traders. It is doubtful that this interpretation of s.92 was intended: the section was to provide a guarantee of free trade, not of free enterprise.[29]

This cautionary tale about constitutionalizing free markets is particularly resonant in the Canadian context because of the change in language proposed by the federal government: from the constitutional directive that goods "be admitted free" into each of the provinces (directed at customs duties) to the declaration that "Canada is an economic union within which persons, goods, services and capital may move freely without barriers or restrictions based on provincial or territorial boundaries" (directed at unrestricted movement).[30] This change of language would be an important signal to the courts, moving us clearly in the direction of the Australian experience.

The constitutionalizing of the common market also has important implications for the role of the judiciary in constitutional litigation. Courts will be called upon to test the economic impact of regulatory measures to determine whether they act as "barriers or restrictions or are saved by the equally vague 'equalization' or 'regional development' exemptions." The 1978 Canadian Bar Association report was sanguine about this prospect: "the courts would find sufficient leeway, as they have done under section 121, to allow for departures from the principle of free movement when need be ... "[31] Again, the Australian experience is instructive. The High Court of Australia wrote that in 1988:

> judicial exegesis of the section (92) has yielded neither clarity of meaning nor certainty of operation. Over the years the court has moved uneasily between one interpretation and another in its endeavours to solve the problems thrown up by the necessity to apply the very general language of the section to a wide variety of legislative and factual situations. Indeed, these shifts have been such as to make it difficult to speak of the section as having achieved a settled or accepted interpretation at any time since federation.[32]

As it would seem that, *prima facie*, any regulatory measure is intended to "distort" the operation of the free market, most measures would be *prima facie* challengeable under the proposed section 121.[33] While the courts are unlikely to strike down every such measure, there will be a great deal of uncertainty in regard to many measures and some that we value will probably not survive. More important, this has significant implications for democratic politics; legislators may be less likely to intervene in the marketplace and, when they do, they may choose to "harmonize downwards"[34] so as to level the playing field. Rather than risk litigation, and facing pressure to retain their competitive advantage *vis à vis* other provinces,[35] governments would be inclined to favour the free market, rather than "distort" it. As Peter Leslie describes it, this version of economic liberalism calls for the "shrinking of the role of government altogether. It is a response to the voices calling for minimal interference in the allocation of resources through market forces."[36]

This may be seen as a valuable outcome for some; for others, it valorizes capitalism over democratic self-rule. The sovereignty of the people acting through their democratically elected representatives will be severely diminished.[37] The saving of laws by declaring them to be in the national interest, and the new proposed federal power to make laws for the efficient functioning of the economic union — both requiring the stringent amending formula standard of "seven and 50" — are strait-jacket substitutes for the free operation of the democratic process.[38]

Winners and Losers

The federal strategy appears to have been to load up the constitutional plate with a variety of wide-ranging proposals, each of which could have substantial implications for the future of the country, united or not. The common market proposals sustain the perception that this round of constitutional negotiations is for all of Canada, not just for Québec. And the Canadian public is legitimately entitled to ask who wins and who loses according to the economic proposals.

At the very least, with the removal of agricultural marketing boards and subsidies on the prairies, it "is most likely that western Canada would lose a large number of farm communities and farm operations ... One would expect much bigger farm operations and fewer farm/rural towns."[39] If there are significant economic losses, we might wish to buffer those losses, as the de Grandpré Commission which looked into the effects of Canada-U.S. free trade was supposed to accomplish in regard to the free trade agreement.[40] Even then, the federal government failed to act. Indeed, Canadians would be justified in asking, given their far-reaching implications, why the common market proposals are part of a package with a very tight time frame which restricts opportunity for in-depth consideration.

To whatever extent barriers to interprovincial trade deserve to be addressed, that should be attempted at the intergovernmental, and not the constitutional, level.[41] Parliamentary and legislative committees should be commissioned to look into a code of conduct designed to address the specific barriers which act as socially indefensible impediments to trade. Redress for unjustifiable barriers should be had before bodies other than courts.

Although part of the "national unity" package, the constitutionalizing of the free market model marks another turn towards the kind of class conflict that characterized the free trade debate. The Business Council on National Issues, the Fraser and C. D. Howe Institutes, and the Canadian Manufacturers' Association will be pitted against the labour movement and against those who are unable to participate freely in the market, such as women and the poor.

The proposals may have another interesting effect. Much of the support for sovereignty within Québec has been led by the new economic élites, who gained financially by the upsurge in Québec economic activity in the 1970s and 1980s.[42] Coupled with the green light from Wall Street for Québec to go it alone economically, they, rather than the poets, musicians and academics, have been calmly leading public opinion in Québec in the march towards sovereignty. The common market proposals are both a lure and a challenge to those élites. Either they will choose the federalist option, with its promise of economic prosperity in a common market, or they will choose to maintain "Québec Inc.," where the National Assembly maintains its close ties to economic development in the province, unhampered by constitutional prohibitions against provincial intrusion into the marketplace. If they choose the market option, the federal strategy may have succeeded in dismembering the sovereignist alliance. If they choose the Québec option, Canadians outside of Québec may then be led, perhaps dangerously, to the brink where rhetoric and reality may not be readily distinguishable.

Chapter 6
The Economic Union
Andrew Jackson

The links between the economy and the state are central to Canadian federalism. The respective roles of the federal and provincial governments are jealously guarded by each.

The intent of the federal proposal to eliminate internal economic barriers to movements of goods, capital, services and labour was to promote economic union within Canada, but it could well have more far-reaching consequences. In this chapter, Andrew Jackson shows that if such measures restricted the ability of provinces to intervene in the economy they could lead to increased north-south integration and weaken the east-west links of the national economy. Canadian economic history suggests that provincial action is required to promote needed economic diversification.

North-south economic integration is now much more powerful and important than east-west economic integration. The major Canadian resource and manufacturing industries — lumber, pulp and paper, mining and smelting, auto, aerospace, communications equipment — are largely oriented towards foreign (particularly U.S.) markets, while smaller service sector companies tend to be primarily oriented to the province in which they are based rather than to the national market as a whole. Economic links between provinces tend to be stronger at the centre (for example, between Ontario and Québec) and weaker at the periphery (for example, between British Columbia and Ontario, or between Nova Scotia and New Brunswick). Trade links between Atlantic Canada and Western Canada are of minimal importance.

The clear danger is that constitutional provisions intended to prevent the creation of internal (within Canada) barriers to trade and investment and to promote economic union may tie the hands of the provinces when it comes to managing the dominant north-south dimension. For example, British Columbia may wish to restrict the export of raw logs in order to force Japanese and U.S. buyers to locate manufacturing facilities in the province. But this probably would be construed as an internal barrier to trade despite the fact that few B.C. logs are shipped to other provinces. To take another example, the common market clause could be used to restrict provincial subsidies and tax incentives in support of economic diversification and development. And yet these are generally intended not so much to discriminate against out-of-province companies as to build provincially based productive capacity so as to participate on better terms in the continental and even global market. Data provided by the Economic Council of Canada in its 1991 annual review, *A Joint Venture: The Economics of Constitutional Options*, show that 20.2 percent of Ontario's total output of goods and services is exported to foreign markets (17.7 percent to the United States), more than the 17.4 percent of total output sold to all provinces outside Ontario. British Columbia exports 18.1 percent of its total output to other countries, and just 12.4 percent to other provinces. Québec is more dependent on sales to other provinces than on sales to other countries (20.2 percent versus 14.6 percent), but the export share has increased significantly in recent years.

Dependence on foreign markets relative to provincial markets is especially pronounced in the manufacturing sector. As the Economic Council data show, Ontario manufacturing is almost twice as dependent upon the U.S. market as upon all provinces outside Ontario combined (31.3 percent versus 17.2 percent of manufacturing shipments). B.C. manufacturers ship 35.4 percent of their output to other countries compared to just 13.5 percent to other provinces. In Québec, by contrast, provincial markets (26.5 percent of shipments) are still more important than export markets (21.3 percent of shipments).

The weakness of east-west integration relative to north-south integration is further borne out by data on the distribution of total corporate revenues. Of all Ontario corporate revenues, 31.2 percent are controlled by foreign companies, compared to just 10 percent controlled by out-of-province companies. (The balance, controlled by Ontario companies, is 58.8 percent.) A total of 24.7 percent of B.C. corporate revenues are controlled by foreign companies, compared to the 18 percent controlled by out-of-province companies.

The internal market is still a vital and important part of the Canadian economic structure, and access to the total Canadian market is important for many sectors, including manufacturing, but especially transportation, financial services, and retail and other services. However, it is the greater strength of north-south ties that we must look to in an assessment of the federal constitutional proposals regarding the economic union.

Given the highly regional nature of the Canadian economy, the strength of north-south economic linkages, and the severity of the current economic crisis (caused in large part by continental integration and the abandonment of positive economic policies on the part of the federal government), it is desirable that the provincial governments be given the scope to play an active economic policy role. Regulating the use of resources to promote industrial diversification and development should be encouraged rather than restricted. The same goes for provincial attempts to organize and mobilize capital for locally based ventures and industrial restructuring through public pension funds, public subsidies, tax incentives and other means. The provinces should also be encouraged to organize public sector procurement to build industrial capacity. To be sure, such policies would best be pursued in a concerted way by the federal and provincial governments, but nothing useful is achieved by tying the provinces' hands at a time when the federal government is totally unwilling to provide real economic leadership.

The key point is that provincial governments intervene in economies which are primarily structured along the north-south axis, as opposed to the east-west axis. This has been true in important respects since the 1920s, and is certainly the dominant reality today. An important lesson of Canadian economic history has been that provincial action is *required* to regulate these north-south linkages, in the interests of economic development and diversification.

Tying the Hands of Government?

The pure economic case for the removal of trade barriers is by no means as simple or clear-cut as is often implied. Most economists would agree that a larger market tends to promote greater efficiency and economies of scale.

For example, small breweries or wire and cable plants serving relatively small provincial markets may be "inefficient" compared to larger plants serving several provinces. But the economic models which project gains from free trade assume full employment: workers displaced from the "inefficient" breweries and wire and cable plants are assumed to find jobs. This assumption is demonstrably untrue in an economy with double-digit unemployment, and pure internal free trade is likely to lead to significant job losses in the short term at least. The example of the Canada-U.S. free trade agreement (FTA) gives no grounds for optimism that these labour adjustment problems would be satisfactorily addressed by the federal government.

Further, the elimination of interprovincial barriers may simply result in gains for companies with a monopoly position, rather than gains for the economy as a whole. This would occur if the dismantling of provincial agricultural marketing boards left farmers vulnerable to a few very large food processing companies, as could well be the case in Atlantic Canada.

In practice, an important distinction has to be made between policies which are explicitly discriminatory (for example, preference for in-province contractors) and policies which are neutral but may have a discriminatory impact (such as, consumer and environmental standards). Even more important, one must distinguish between overtly discriminatory policies and policies which are positive interventions in a market economy designed to secure public policy objectives.

From a purely economic "free market" viewpoint, a wide range of positive governmental economic and even social policy initiatives are viewed as discriminatory because they alter the outcomes that would otherwise occur in a market economy. An orthodox "free market" economist would argue that a subsidy is equivalent in impact and even in intent to a trade barrier. For example, a requirement that Ontario Hydro buy wire and cable in Ontario is little different from a provincial subsidy to Ontario wire and cable plants. The courts might well agree.

Virtually all provinces provide subsidies, tax concessions, soft loans or preferential utility rates to companies operating in their jurisdiction in order to actively promote economic diversification and development. Alberta has used the Alberta Heritage Trust Fund to provide developmental capital under favourable terms and conditions to Alberta-based companies. Québec has used the Caisse de dépôt et placement — made up of QPP and public sector pension funds — as a means of promoting the development of Québec-based companies. It has recently provided highly concessionary hydro rates to attract new smelters to the province. Ontario provides enhanced research and development tax credits to Ontario-based companies. The list is almost endless.

The new section 121 proposed for the constitution prohibits laws and practices that constitute barriers to the mobility of capital. Would such a section lead the courts to strike down positive governmental initiatives that favour companies based in a particular province? The answer is by no means certain, but policies that alter the allocation of production between the provinces (and are thus discriminatory and market distorting from the point of view of orthodox economists and neo-conservative politicians) would probably be viewed as such by the courts. Certainly many experts in Québec fear that the proposed clause could be used to undermine the instruments of positive state intervention such as the Caisse which have been built up in that province over the past two decades.

It is possible that the proposed strengthened economic union clause could also be used to strike down or restrict the power of the provinces to control resources. For example, Alberta requires that provincial government approval be given for exports of oil and gas to another province. The clause may also have implications for the pricing policies of provincial hydroelectric and other utilities which discriminate in favour of provincial residents and businesses. There are also potential implications for provincial public auto insurance companies, since a public monopoly could be said to be a barrier to interprovincial trade. (A British Columbia motorist cannot buy auto insurance from an Ontario insurance company.) Like the FTA, the economic union clause would make difficult or impossible the creation of new public enterprises.

It is not only provincial policies that could be vulnerable to a strengthened section 121. Certain federal policies could (and have been) interpreted to interfere with the free movement of goods, services, capital and labour. While equalization and regional development programmes are specifically exempted, extended regional unemployment insurance benefits and specific regional transportation subsidies could be seen to be discriminatory.

The exception proposed by the federal government for purposes of regional development is quite restrictive. It would seem that if Newfoundland, for example, wished to give preference to local companies and local workers in offshore oil development, it would have to have the project declared by Parliament to be in the national interest, and this would have to be supported by seven provinces with 50 percent of the population. Effectively, then, the use of this tool for regional economic development would be seriously curtailed. Moreover, this exception means that the federal government would have an effective veto over provincial government actions which, as things now stand, are within the provinces' constitutional competence. This would probably in turn be used to secure a rapid dismantling of most existing provincial "barriers" and to put a brake upon the activities of economically interventionist provincial governments.

The proposed economic union clause can also be seen as a means of giving greater effect to restrictions on government policies contained within the Canada-U.S. free trade agreement. For example, if Ontario were to require Ontario hospitals to give preference to Ontario-made medical equipment, this would be in violation of the FTA. As things stand now, the FTA would have to be enforced by the federal government, whose power to act in this respect is far from clear or certain. This gives Ontario a certain amount of leeway. The constitutional proposal means that such a requirement on Ontario's part would be unconstitutional, and thus would be struck down by the courts.

And, finally, it is ironic indeed that the proposals for a closer economic union are combined in the constitutional package with a proposal to give up federal jurisdiction in training, an area which is intimately bound up with the issue of labour mobility within the economic union. In practice, federal involvement in training is much more likely to promote national skills certification (an important dimension of mobility) than is the alternative of interprovincial agreement. Further, the provinces are less likely to be interested in training for the full range of potential job opportunities available in the national labour market than is the federal government. Exclusive provincial jurisdiction over training carries the very real risk that workers will receive non-portable qualifications and skills, making moves from one provincial labour market to another much more difficult. In addressing this issue, it is important to bear in mind that there are significant differences between the Québec labour market and the overall Canadian labour market. But a general devolution of power over training to the provinces could weaken the ability of citizens to acquire the skills they need to take an active part in the economic life of Canada.

In conclusion, constitutional proposals regarding the economic union should be examined in terms of their potential impact upon the abilities of government to intervene in the economy, shape the market, and affect market outcomes. Proposals which bind the capacity of governments to intervene ultimately sacrifice democracy. In the name of market efficiency, much that is important to citizen well-being is lost.

Chapter 7

A National Government in a Federal State

A. W. Johnson

If the provinces have played an important role in fostering economic development, the role of the federal government has, if anything, been more significant. But the idea of devolving powers to the provinces was at the centre of the Meech Lake proposals. It is still very much an issue in constitutional negotiations.

In this excerpt from a longer document, A. W. Johnson argues that Canada could be significantly weakened if the role of the national government is not fully recognized in constitutional reform. He makes the case that a strong national government does not have to exclude a unique, non-preferential arrangement for Québec, and focuses on the weakening of federal authority that would result from the Mulroney-Clark proposals.

One central question must be asked about the 1991 Mulroney-Clark constitutional proposals. Will they lead once again in the direction that has been seen to fail in the past: special status for Québec or will they lead to a major devolution of powers from the federal to the provincial governments?

The dilemma is well known to Canadians. Québec, on the one hand, is insisting upon a massive devolution of powers from the government of Canada to the government of Québec — whether by way of a devolution of powers to Québec alone, or by a similar devolution to all the provinces. Canadians outside of Québec, on the other hand, have rejected both these courses of action. They have opposed special status for Québec on the grounds that no province should enjoy a preferential position in Canada. And they have opposed any significant weakening of Canada's national government, particularly given the global pressures Canada now confronts. Western and Atlantic Canadians, indeed, want "into" a strong national government, not "out of" it: this is why they are seeking equal, or at least more nearly equal, representation in a reformed and elected Senate. This, however, is a reform Québec politicians have always rejected.

What to do? Either Québec must give up its demands or greatly attenuate them; or Canadians outside Québec must give up their opposition to a special status for Québec or to a significantly weakened national government. Perhaps Canadians must even give up their advocacy of a seriously reformed Senate. The most obvious alternative to these options is for the government of Canada to try to finesse its way through to *some* weakening of the national government, *some* special status for Québec, and *some* Senate reform that might be grudgingly accepted by Québecers and Canadians outside Québec — whether through persuasion, or confusion about the proposals, or constitutional fatigue, or fear of the consequences of not doing so.

Mulroney and Clark and their colleagues have chosen the latter course. And the question is whether the some-of-everything they have proposed will be enough (for the one side) or too much (for the other side).

Only a careful analysis of the 1991 federal proposals will provide an answer to this question. For the proposals are not only wide-ranging and detailed, but even more confusingly, they are not identified with, or grouped around, the issues which they really are addressing — namely, those that are raised by the Canada-Québec dilemma.

The most serious difficulties with the Mulroney-Clark proposals begin with division of the powers between the federal and provincial governments. The burden of these proposals is to weaken the national government very considerably in several distinct ways.

Delegation of Legislative Powers

The first proposal is that federal and provincial governments should be given the power to decide among themselves — one by one or together — how the powers of governing Canada should be divided up, *de facto*. This would be achieved through the delegation of legislative powers: the government of Canada could choose (or be persuaded) to delegate certain of its powers to legislate to one or more provinces, or the governments of the provinces could choose to delegate certain of their powers to the national government. There would be two limits on this power of delegation: first, Parliament and the provincial legislature, or legislatures, would have to ratify any such agreement between the prime minister and the premier(s); and, second, the government that delegated the power would be able, constitutionally, to revoke its delegation.

This proposal may look innocuous, and its goal of greater harmony between governments is very appealing. In reality, however, it is fraught with grave dangers.

The first of them has to do with the process that is proposed for transferring powers from the federal government to the provinces, or vice versa: it is essentially a process of "deal making." All that is required is deciding which government should have the power to "do a deal" between the prime minister and one or more premiers, followed by legislative ratification. This is tantamount to the constitutionalization of the Meech Lake process — but without any requirement for a constitutional consensus across Canada.

The second danger has to do with the results that would, or could, flow from the process. There is little doubt, in my view, that this method of dividing up legislative powers would result in a substantial weakening of federal powers. These, after all, are the powers that have been under assault by the provinces for the last two decades, and they are the powers that Québec nationalists are seeking. Strong prime ministers and strong governments would resist, of course, but Canadians know full well there is no guarantee that the nation's political parties will always be led by strong people. The potential is very real, therefore, that this "deal-making" power would weaken the nation's capacity to address questions regarding the environment, social policy, transportation and communications, or any other federal power under dispute. This is reason enough to reject this proposal — but there are more.

A third potential result of the proposed legislative delegation power can readily be divined. It would be possible, under the federal proposals, for the government of Canada to delegate some of its powers to some of the provinces — those that were demanding them —

but to retain those powers in respect of the rest of the provinces. More than that, some provinces might persuade the federal government to take over some of their responsibilities (for example, the more costly ones). The consequence would be that Parliament's legislation would come to apply to some of the provinces and not to others and that this asymmetry in the application of federal legislation would differ as between different fields of government. In the end the public would lose all track of which government was responsible and accountable for what. This would spell the end of true electoral accountability. Canada would have hodgepodge federalism.

It can be argued, of course, that these are doomsday scenarios. It cannot, however, be argued that they are *not* possible, nor can it be argued that provincial pressure for more powers, and in particular Québec pressure, for more powers will cease. The sheer realities of Canada, in short, force one to the conclusion that if governments could transfer powers between themselves there would be only one certain result: a weakening of the powers of Parliament, and the weakening of the public's respect for Parliament.

The Spending Power and the Residual Power

The second way in which the Mulroney-Clark proposals would weaken the national government would be by disabling the spending power of Parliament, and by weakening the clause in the constitution that gives Parliament the right to legislate in areas not specifically assigned to the provinces.

The spending power, and its use by Parliament, is what made medicare possible, what enabled the federal financing of Canada's universities and colleges, what made the Canada Council possible, and what gives Parliament the power to contribute to the poor through the Canada Assistance Plan. But it is a power that is deeply resented in Québec, and is from time to time opposed by the other provinces on the grounds that it enables Parliament to spend in areas of exclusive provincial jurisdiction.

To meet these objections, the Mulroney-Clark proposals would require a national consensus on future uses of the spending power. The consensus suggested is the assent of seven provinces representing a majority of the Canadian people. The idea of a national consensus is reasonable, in my view, given the potential for arbitrary uses of the spending power. What is *not* reasonable, however, is the use of the Meech Lake process for determining the consensus — the ten premiers plus the prime minister, "alone in a room." Substitute for this a referendum across Canada, and require the assent of the people in seven provinces representing 50 percent of Canada's population, and the proposal makes sense in democratic, political and constitutional terms.

It is not the consensus requirement, however, that cripples the spending power. It is the further proposal that the provinces that choose not to participate in new national programmes (under the spending power) would be entitled to federal compensation, providing they launched programmes that met the "objectives" of the new programme. Not the principles, or the criteria, or the standards of the new programme; only its objectives. In my view, this would mean, effectively, that there would be no new national programmes.

There is one good and simple reason for saying this. Every premier and every provincial minister of finance would have a no-lose incentive for opting out: they would be compensated by the federal government whether or not they conformed with the norms and the standards of the proposed national programme. They would be in a position to get at least some "free money" for other objectives simply by mounting a less costly programme, and they would avoid any real accountability for the spending of the "equivalent compensation" they got from the federal government. The probability, therefore, of a federal programme being adopted by enough provinces that it could be launched as a truly national programme, is so slim that no government of Canada would be likely to try to start one. These opting-out incentives would be weakened, of course, if the compensation were to be paid to the *people* of opting-out provinces by way of tax credits, rather than to the *governments*. To do this would be far more logical. After all, the people of the province that has opted out would continue to pay the same federal taxes as before, but they would no longer benefit from one of the programmes being financed by those taxes. So they are the ones who should get a refund.

If these two changes were made to the federal proposal on the spending power — the referendum on its use, and the compensation to people instead of governments — I think most Canadians would accept the limitation on its use. Not so in Québec, however. At least it is not likely. Québec politicians have consistently pressed either for a complete abolition of the spending power, or at least for the right to opt out with full compensation going to the provincial government.

The federal proposal to weaken the peace, order and good government clause in the constitution — the one that gives Parliament the power to legislate in areas that are not specifically assigned to the provinces — would work in a different way. The courts have in the past relied on this clause to uphold the power of Parliament to legislate in areas where jurisdiction is unclear — such as the environment, for example — on the grounds that Parliament can legislate in matters where there are clear "national dimensions." (This is known as the "residual power.") The Mulroney-Clark proposals would open up to dispute the question of what *is* a national dimension by saying in the constitution that Parliament could not legislate on "non-national" matters. The question could arise, for example, in respect of environmental issues that affect two prairie provinces, the Rafferty-Alameda Dam being a case in point. Whether this change would in fact make a difference in judicial interpretations of the constitution is, of course, a matter of judgement. The question to be asked is what the purpose of this proposal is in the first place, if it is *not* designed to weaken federal powers.

Weakening the Federal Role in Specific Areas of Government

In addition to their general weakening of the powers of Parliament — by the delegation of legislative powers, and by changes to the spending power and the peace, order and good government clause — the federal proposals would also potentially weaken the role of the government of Canada in certain specific areas of government.

The first and the most important of these is labour-market training (usually called manpower training). Having said that "labour-market training is the key to Canada's future prosperity," the government promptly turned around and said that it should be recognized as an area of exclusive provincial jurisdiction. True, it suggested that the national government should have the power to set "standards and objectives." But this would be contingent on the provinces' agreeing to give Ottawa the power to do so. And even if the provinces did agree, once the government of Canada had drafted the "standards and objectives," they would not become operative unless seven provinces representing at least 50 percent of the population agreed to them. Presumably, too, the dissenting provinces would have the right to opt out. The real role of the government of Canada, in short, would be tenuous.

The second set of powers that would be shifted from the federal government to the provinces — also on the *economic activity* side of the division of powers — would be forestry, mining and tourism. These, too, would be declared to be under exclusive provincial jurisdiction, subject only to "the preservation of Canada's existing research and development capacity, [and] obligations for international and native affairs." (We are not told how that would be achieved.)

There are, however, certain other national concerns on which the government of Canada may well want to act in these fields. One has to do with any global economic strategy that might be developed in the future: Would these areas of economic activity have to be excluded from that strategy (if the strategy went any further than exhortation)? Another has to do with the environment: Would the declaration that mining and forestry are matters of exclusive provincial jurisdiction put them beyond Parliament's power to pass environmental legislation (which has been supported up until now by the courts)? This is what the courts would have to decide. As for tourism, the question is whether the federal government's interest in the contribution of tourism to the balance of payments, and to economic activity generally, is sufficient to justify some doubt about the proposed surrender of that field to the provinces.

On the *social* side of the distribution of powers, the Mulroney-Clark proposals would have the government of Canada withdraw from any activity in the field of housing — which means, of course, that the Central Mortgage and Housing Corporation would go. As to social policy generally, the 1991 proposals contained, as more than one premier noted, no provision for any affirmation of social rights in the constitution.

On the *cultural* side of the division of powers, the government proposed that national cultural institutions — the government calls them "Canada-wide" institutions, not national ones — should be maintained. But it suggested that every province should have the right to negotiate agreements with Ottawa under which the role of the federal government in that province would be defined. The Mulroney-Clark proposals assumed that "the current sharing of responsibilities ... may be appropriate in most provinces" but that the government of Québec would seek different arrangements. The agreements thus negotiated on a bilateral basis would then be "constitutionalized." Once again, we see the Meech Lake process of constitutional amendment.

The same kind of formulation would apply to immigration — that increasingly difficult and contentious issue in nearly every developed country in the world. Under the Mulroney-Clark proposals, the government of Canada would retain its power to determine the total number of immigrants, and to set "national standards and objectives related to immigration." But it would negotiate bilateral agreements with any province that wanted a stronger role for itself.

The fundamental question, of course, in respect of all the *specific* powers that would be turned over to the provinces under the Mulroney-Clark proposals is how much they would tilt the balance in Québec, and in

Canada outside of Québec, for or against the proposals on the division of powers proposals, taken as a whole.

What *is* clear, in my view, is that when you put the several Mulroney-Clark proposals on the division of powers together, they *do* significantly weaken Canada's national government: by permitting the provincial and federal governments to come to a new division of powers by negotiation; by curtailing the federal spending power and limiting the residual power; and, by weakening, however moderately, the federal government's role in other specified areas of economic, social and cultural activity.

A Whole New Approach to Constitutional Reform

The fallacy underlying these proposals for a general devolution of powers is the proposition that every provincial government must be offered whatever powers the Québec government may be offered. Which means it becomes quite impossible to accommodate Québec's demands without at the same time weakening the national government.

Now, this proposition derives from an entirely legitimate principle, namely that all provinces must be equal in their constitutional powers. But unfortunately it is not a correct interpretation of that principle. In truth it is the constitutional powers of the *people* of every province that must be equal — which is to say, the powers they may exercise through their provincial governments, plus those they may exercise through their MPs and Senators in Parliament. For surely the Constitution is meant to serve the people of Canada, not their governments.

If this is so, there are two ways of achieving equality in the constitutional powers available to the people of Canada. One is to maintain equality in the constitutional powers assigned to provincial governments, plus equality in the constitutional powers of the MPs and Senators from every province. The other way is to permit the people of one or more provinces to enjoy reduced constitutional powers in Parliament, by way of their MPs and Senators, in favour of increased constitutional powers for their provincial governments.

It follows that under this construction of the equality principle, it is possible to establish a different status for one province (or, theoretically, more) without disturbing the constitutional arrangements as they apply to other provinces, and to do so without granting any special, or preferential status.

There is, in short, a second way to resolve Canada's constitutional dilemma. Transfer certain of Parliament's powers to Québec's National Assembly, but provide that wherever Parliament cannot constitutionally legislate in Québec (the areas transferred), Québec MPs and Senators can no longer legislate in the rest of Canada, through Parliament. They would simply lose their power to speak or to vote on the specific measures that could not, constitutionally, apply in Québec. This would not apply to Appropriation Acts or taxation measures: they have to do with the ensemble of government functions. As to the specific measures themselves (in respect of which Québec's MPs and Senators could not participate), the government would have to find support for its measures from among the MPs and Senators from other provinces. If the government failed, and were defeated on its measures, that defeat would not be treated as a no-confidence vote.

The consequence of this approach to constitutional reform is, of course, striking. The people of Québec could have more constitutional powers through their provincial government than would the people of the other provinces, but they would enjoy correspondingly less power than the others, through their MPs and Senators in Parliament. (They would have to understand, too, that if whole functions of government were transferred to Québec, such, for example, as health and social security, they could not expect to have a Québecer as minister in charge of that function.) Taken together, however, the constitutional powers that would be exercised by Québecers would be equal those enjoyed by Canadians elsewhere. No special status for anyone, in short.

This is a far more hopeful answer to Canada's constitutional dilemma than the conventional one: it enables Canadians outside of Québec to maintain the strong national government they want, while at the same time accommodating Québec in its demands. This surely is the approach the Government of Canada should be following — not an approach under which the whole of Canada must lose in its effort to keep Québec in the federation.

Chapter 8

Failing to Meet Regional Needs

Michael Bradfield

One of the main features of the Canadian economy is the existence of wide disparities in income, employment and production among the regions. This argues for flexibility in policy making to allow for regionally specific measures. But the 1991 federal proposals included an economic package that suggested generally applicable economic policies. These included measures to co-ordinate federal and provincial fiscal policies and to give primacy to inflation fighting as a mandate for the Bank of Canada, as well as to promote further economic integration.

Michael Bradfield argues that, taken together, these measures would promote a central Canadian bias in economic policy and neglect the needs of the poorer regions of Canada. He shows that the arguments advanced in their favour are based on dubious assumptions and questionable research.

Canada has serious national economic problems, not the least of which are its chronic regional disparities. These regional disparities reflect the very different economic bases of Canada's regions. The low-income, high-unemployment regions are generally resource based. Where agriculture is important, a region is subject to the instabilities of weather and prices. Where raw materials are important, the regional economy often suffers from declining demand and prices. As the long-term effects of the post-industrial economy accumulate, such economies are likely to need even greater stimulus. Meanwhile, the provinces most likely to benefit from the changing structure of the economy are Ontario and Québec: they are the most highly urbanized provinces and they contain both the nation's manufacturing and its research and development bases.

The 1991 Mulroney-Clark economic proposals for harmonizing provincial and federal fiscal policies, for removing all interprovincial barriers to factor (capital and labour) and goods flows, and for limiting the Bank of Canada to fighting inflation showed a fundamental misunderstanding of the Canadian economy and a misreading of the mood of the nation. The government's claim that the benefits could be as high as $16,000 per family cannot be substantiated — the upper limit would be about $450.[1]

Both the short- and long-term needs of Canada's hinterlands will differ from each other and from the centre. To suggest the harmonization of provincial with national policies is, at best, to turn a blind eye to the nature and needs of the hinterlands. At worst, it is an indirect method of forcing people from the hinterlands to the centre: the "nation-building" focus of the federal proposals could mean destroying some of the regions.

The federal government and the Bank of Canada must take responsibility for the economic welfare of the entire country and of the separate regions. Since these often conflict, these federal decision makers must inevitably trade off conflicting interests or else they must develop regionally sensitive fiscal and monetary policies. They have been generally unwilling to do the latter, particularly for monetary policy. Therefore we have grown accustomed to seeing federal policies that harm some of the regions most of the time, in the name of the greater (national) good. Even the best-intentioned federal government may make the wrong choice in terms of trade-offs or policy. An ideologically driven government such as we now have cannot be counted on to be "best intentioned" and therefore is even more likely to make the wrong choices. The provinces need the capacity to shield themselves from such policy choices.

The economic package released with the federal government's 1991 proposals emphasized the importance of total interprovincial economic integration for our future prosperity, and even for our sense of citizenship.[2] However, Canada is already a highly integrated, although regionally disparate, economy and there are only very minor gains (probably about one-half of 1 percent of GNP) to be made from complete integration. But complete integration would further restrict the capacity of the provinces to affect their own economies. The complete mobility of labour, capital and products would constrain the provinces' ability to introduce their own tax régimes, and the harmonization of provincial with federal fiscal policy would restrict the ability of provinces to expand demand. Integration is therefore a serious bone of contention tossed into the constitutional fray. With so little to gain for the national economy and so much to lose in the provincial economies and in the resolution of our constitutional crisis, one can only speculate as to the thinking behind the proposals.

The Federal Proposals

The increases in output from greater integration projected by the federal government were vastly overstated; these were then multiplied by two to come up with the impact on the average Canadian family. In addition, the costs of integration in terms of job loss and dislocation, decreased competition in the Canadian economy, and a potential lowering of standards for the environment, for worker safety and for business behaviour were ignored or assumed to be benefits.

European estimates of the benefits *to them* of their own integration were cited, with an increase in incomes of 11.5 to 16.5 percent, of which five to ten percentage points derive from monetary union alone.[3] These estimates were then applied to Canada, claiming a gain in living standards, for a presumably average Canadian family of four, of $11 000 to $16 000 per year! Such gains are so impressive that *The Financial Post* carried them without critical comment.[4]

These estimates do not bear close scrutiny. In the first place, Canada is not moving to a monetary union; we are one. Thus, five to ten percentage points of the European Community gains cannot be applied to Canada. In addition, the European Community of 1992 will be bringing those countries into an integrated economy similar to what Canada already has. The gains we still have to achieve are minor improvements given our already high level of integration — much higher than the Europe of 1991. Thus, we cannot expect to make even the 6.5 percent increase in incomes predicted from integration in Europe.

Finally, the gain for a family of four was overestimated even further because the gain was based on an average income of $100 000, for whom an 11 percent gain leads to an increase of $11 000.[5] Perhaps this reflects the average income of those who wrote the document, but it is roughly twice the income of the average Canadian family.

So what would be a reasonable estimate of the gain from integration? While admitting that the effects are difficult to measure, the federal government claimed that "efforts to quantify existing costs point to a significant national economic burden" and cited both the Macdonald Royal Commission and the Canadian Manufacturers' Association (CMA).[6] The government did not admit that the Macdonald background studies note that "the direct economic costs of internal barriers to trade in Canada are quite small: removing them would not result in dramatic economic gains."[7] Other studies done for the Macdonald Commission also estimate small gains, usually of less than 1 percent.[8]

The federal report failed to note that the Macdonald Royal Commission studies warned that their statistical methods required heroic assumptions and therefore the estimates should be "treated with caution."[9] The models used in the Macdonald studies often assumed perfectly competitive markets. More realistic market assumptions would reduce the gains from integration still further. The CMA figure of slightly less than 1 percent is unsubstantiated and differs dramatically from Hazeldine's estimates, which go as low as one-tenth of 1 percent.[10]

Even if we engage in a willing suspension of disbelief and accept 1 percent as an upper estimate of the gains from integration, the effect would be to increase the average family income, in 1990 dollars, by only $450. Thus the earlier estimate of the federal paper exceeds this upper estimate by a factor of 35.5 (16 000/450). It should be noted that to lower the unemployment rate by only one percentage point would increase growth by 2.5

percent, a far greater gain than any reasonable estimate of the gains from further integration.

The dishonesty of the federal proposal extends from vastly overstating the benefits of integration to totally ignoring the costs. The primary cost of further integration of the Canadian economy internally, and with the United States through the free trade agreement, is the dislocation of labour because of the jobs which will be lost to competition from outside. And even small gains in total employment that may result may be accompanied by a significant displacement of workers. In addition, economies of scale — one of the benefits claimed from integration — aggravate "the incidence and severity of adjustments";[11] therefore, "the blithe dismissal of adjustment pressure" is not warranted.[12]

The federal government does not see the loss of jobs as a real cost but as simply the loss of a "perceived" benefit.[13] Nonetheless, job loss is a real cost to the individuals whose firm or industry is destroyed by outside competition. Unemployment is a serious cost to the provinces whose social assistance payments and training costs (a responsibility to be transferred to them under these proposals) go up and whose tax revenues go down. There is also a real cost to the whole economy as output is lost when more jobs are eliminated in an economy already suffering excessive unemployment. Thus, these costs are not likely to be short-term transitional problems.

There are other costs which are ignored by the Mulroney-Clark proposals. It is assumed that integrating the Canadian and U.S. economies will lead to increased competition and lower prices. But if there are economies of scale to be achieved, this will not only mean fewer jobs but fewer companies and less effective competition in specific markets. If integration is accompanied by deregulation on the theory that competition will be increased, this shows an inability to learn from history and incompetence at applying theory. It would, nonetheless, be totally consistent with this government's economic and political and social agenda.

Finally, integration may lead to a dilution of occupational safety and health, environmental and social standards as companies use their increased mobility to force provinces to adopt the lowest prevailing standards. To ignore the increased power that corporations will have in dealing with provinces, especially the small, lagging provinces, is to ignore the realities of the marketplace, however much it fits the ideology of the government.

One of the repeated claims made by the federal government in its policy paper is that these proposals are an attempt to achieve greater "transparency" or openness in policy making, because "Canadians do not have a sufficient awareness of the objectives and intentions of governments, nor of the economic and fiscal pressures they face ... "[14] If this is true, why are Canadians being misled about the benefits of integration? Could it be that Canadians want a "less transparent" — that is, a constitutional — process, because they have seen that the integration proposal is designed to meet the requirements of the Canada-U.S. trade agreement rather than to enhance the incomes of Canadians?

The government does not mention the significance of the trade agreement, that it gives U.S. firms unhindered access to Canadian markets, in the guise of "national status." Economic integration increases competition from other provinces but also from all of the American states and their powerful corporations.

It is claimed that integration will enhance "our rights of citizenship."[15] When combined with the trade agreement, integration will give the citizens of Québec the same right as the citizens of Kansas, the citizens of British Columbia the same right as those of the District of Columbia: the right to sink or swim in the private marketplace. At the same time, these proposals diminish those rights and values which Canadians prize most highly: government intervention to protect us from the ravages of the unfettered marketplace in the form of a decent medicare programme, the protection of workers' rights and a social safety net. The provincial governments should be upset by the proposals to harmonize the fiscal policies of the provinces with federal government policy. Such proposals suggest that the federal government — or at least the federal government supported by seven provinces representing at least 50 percent of the population — knows best what is good for all of Canada. But this ignores both the separate responsibilities of the levels of government and the highly differentiated economies in Canada's regions.

Provincial governments clearly have a responsibility for the functioning of their own economies. This is especially important for the smaller, peripheral economies whose needs and concerns have received declining federal attention and support in the last decade. These economies have tended to suffer the most from restrictive federal policies. To the extent that federal policies are triggered by major shifts in national statistics or trends, the needs of the smaller and poorer economies are not addressed. Their trends are swamped by those of the larger central economies, and their realities may vary drastically from national signals. What appears reasonable from national statistics may not be appropriate for many, even most, of the provinces.

These and other issues also apply to the federal proposal to harmonize provincial policies with those of the

Bank of Canada. A province has limited means at its disposal for dealing with high unemployment, but this task is made virtually impossible if the Bank of Canada is running a high-interest policy which adds to the province's debt servicing costs, depresses private investment and consumption expenditures, and drives up the value of the Canadian dollar, thereby cutting exports. To expect the smaller, lagging provinces to cut their spending when the Bank of Canada is dampening demand is to ask those provinces to give up all attempts at ameliorating regional disparities.

The need for provincial policy levers is further increased if the proposal for limiting the Bank of Canada to fighting inflation is implemented. In the first place, high interest rates as a tool of fighting inflation make sense only in a full employment economy experiencing excess demand. To the extent that national inflationary pressures are demand driven, they are likely to come from the central region's economy. The rest of the economy may still need expansionary, not contractionary, policies.

When the inflationary pressures are profit driven, they too are likely to come from the centre, because that is where the companies with the economic power to raise domestic prices are concentrated. In this case too, monetary policy is not the appropriate tool, but nonetheless the one many federal governments tend to use. The same would be true of a wage-driven cost increase.

In addition, inflation could result from government policies such as the introduction of the GST or other taxes. Again, to be a significant factor in national inflation, these policies would have to emanate from the largest jurisdictions — the federal government or central Canada. To make all of Canada suffer from high interest rates to control an inflation emanating from the policies of the federal or central provincial governments is to strain the ties that bind.

If inflation is imported, resulting from rising prices elsewhere, monetary policy is unnecessary. The primary inflation concern of most federal governments is with international competitiveness. But externally generated inflation will mean still higher inflation outside the nation than in, so that our international competitiveness would be enhanced, induced internal inflation notwithstanding. Again, a fight against inflation and the use of monetary policy would be harmful and inappropriate in a less than full-employment economy.

Thus, to limit the Bank's mandate to fighting inflation is to commit to a policy that will be generally inappropriate even in the national interest, for full employment for Canada is not in sight. A high-interest-rate policy is even less appropriate for the lagging regions of Canada, and to expect them to harmonize their policies with a tight-money policy is to ask too much. In addition, the federal goal of *zero* inflation is totally unreasonable even as a federal policy. It implies potentially massive unemployment, with a disproportionate amount of the burden carried by the resource-oriented peripheral economies.

To expect provinces to agree to harmonize their policies with federal fiscal and monetary policies while also fully integrating provincial economies is to rub salt in the wounds. Integration would put provincial firms and even industries at risk because of increased competition not only from other provinces, but from the United States, since U.S. firms have equal access under the Canada-U.S. trade agreement. This will exacerbate regional disparities and *increase* the need for provincial responses independent of national fiscal or monetary policies.

It would obviously be misguided for provinces to accept these federal harmonization proposals. It was foolhardy for the federal government to include them in the delicate constitutional discussions. Moreover, it was totally unnecessary to bring banking matters in at this stage, since the changes in the Bank's mandate can be done with federal legislation and are not part of the constitutional package *per se*.

The primary deterrents to higher productivity and global competitiveness in Canada have been federal policies. The federal government's fetish of globalism, the related phobia of inflation and its reliance on monetary policy have led it to drive up interest rates and depress domestic demand. The high-interest-rate policy has attracted foreign funds which have driven up the exchange rate of the Canadian dollar, thereby eroding our global competitiveness. Ironically, because "too much reliance has been placed on restrictive monetary policy in the last decade, we are less competitive as a nation than we could have been with a different policy mix."[16]

Instead of admitting that the high-interest/high-exchange policy was to satisfy U.S. demands for going into the free trade negotiations,[17] this federal policy paper reverses cause and effect by saying that rising government debt led to increased foreign borrowing and therefore to higher interest rates.[18] In reality, it was the jump in interest rates in the early 1980s and again under the Mulroney government which forced provinces to borrow abroad and which raised debt-servicing costs and therefore deficits. The only transparency in this federal paper is its transparently shameless attempt to deflect the blame for the mess the economy is in.

Finally, let us deal with the hypocrisy involved in proposing regional representation on the Bank of

Canada's board of directors. There are already regional appointments to the Bank with no noticeable impact on the Bank's sensitivity to regional problems. The proposed regional consultative panels would have no power, not even a guarantee that they would be listened to. Since the conventional wisdom is that the Bank cannot have regionally sensitive monetary policies, then if the Bank's mandate is limited to controlling inflation, the regional representatives would have little to do but run interferencc for the Bank. Obviously, neither democracy nor regional needs are served by thc regional representation proposal.

The Tory Strategy

The Mulroney government wants to make sure its ideology continues long after its political mandate has ended. The democratic process may well remove this government and party from power for a long time to come, but it would be far more difficult to free ourselves of its policies once they are entrenched in the constitution. And of course, the constitution should not enshrine specific policies but basic and lasting principles.

To have come forward with an economic package which threatens the powers of the provinces was a blunder of immense proportions. There are already too many issues and too many vested interests involved in the constitutional debate. To provide more reasons for argument and rejection is to diminish the probabilities of a rational and successful constitutional debate.

An alternative view might be that the government has expoited the pressure of the constitutional debate in order to piggy-back its economic proposals. This view says that the government is not stupid, just cynical. The prime minister chose a high-risk strategy with the Meech

Lake proposals and failed disastrously. Has he learned nothing? Does he believe the rest of us have learned nothing?

Canadians have a much stronger set of principles, a much clearer sense of democracy, and much higher goals for Canada than the government that produced this document.

Chapter 9
The European Community as Model

George Ross

The European community is often cited in Canadian constitutional debate. The 1992 initiative to create a single market is heralded as an example of new thinking that Canadians cannot ignore. However, it is far from clear that there is any one lesson to be learned from the European experience. George Ross argues that debates within the EC reflect underlying differences in political philosophy between social democrats and neo-liberals (sometimes called neo-conservatives). He shows that the specific features of European integration make it an inappropriate model for Canadian federalism: what Europe and Canada share are the common origins of their economic difficulties dating to the 1980s. He suggests that the European example should convince Canadians of the political importance of institutional change.

The great publicity surrounding "1992," the European Community's highly successful programme to accelerate economic union among its twelve member states has led people in every corner of the globe to propose the Community as a model for linking different national, cultural and economic collectivities. It is not surprising, then, to find the European Community (EC) being proposed, explicitly or implicitly, as a model of constitution writing and economy building for Canada. Canadians should be very careful when they hear this, however, for EC "federalism," such as it is, is profoundly different from Canada's. Moreover, the EC's movement towards "economic union" contrasts with that of Canada in essential ways.

Federalism and Sovereignty

Canada is a long-standing nation state, organized as a federation, that is at present discussing a reconfiguration of different aspects of its constitution. Its problem is to find a new institutional mix which will allow the successful coexistence of different provinces, regions and cultures whose aspirations have changed over time. The European Community, in contrast, is not a nation at all, but rather an international organization founded to foster the integration of separate European societies.

The history of EC constitution building reveals a very tentative approach to federalism. A mere thirty-five years ago there was no EC, just a group of fully sovereign nations whose relationships had been punctuated by bloody conflicts over centuries. The Community, compared to Canada, is thus a political infant whose institutional structures are the product of evolving regional association by the nations of Western Europe. The principle of EC constitution building is revealed by its legal form. The Community's juridical foundation is a set of treaties, contractual arrangements agreed upon among independent actors. Over the EC's brief lifetime its member states have pooled important parts of their sovereignty, but for *specific purposes* only. The Community *cannot act* unless areas and decision rules are explicitly spelled out in treaties. Thus, the 1957 Treaty of Rome and other EC treaties (most recently the 1985 Single European Act, which enshrines the 1992 Single Market Programme) list all Community powers and decision-making procedures. What is not listed (all "residual powers") remains entirely with the member states. Indeed, whether the European Community should be federal, and how much so, has been ferociously disputed from its beginnings to the present. Contemporary battles between federalist Jacques Delors and anti-federalist Margaret Thatcher have been quite as titanic as early disagreements between Jean Monnet and Charles de Gaulle.

The scope of EC federalism has always been circumscribed. The Community began as an experiment in integrating previously separate states and societies. Given the experiment's great complexity, Europe's founders decided to move forward only on strategically chosen problems. Their hope was that success in such limited areas would whet appetites and build confidence for greater expansion later. Thus, for much of its first quarter century the Community was engaged in establishing a customs-free zone inside the EC's external borders, erecting a common external tariff around this zone and elaborating the Common Agricultural Policy, which currently causes so many difficulties for international trade. Within these areas, if policy proposals were usually made by the Community's Commission — which the Treaty of Rome designated as EC policy initiator and executive — all decisions to enact Commission proposals had to be made by the Council of Ministers of EC member states agreeing unanimously. EC federalism was thus constrained within a broader confederal structure. Even in those few areas where the Commission could propose, any member state could veto what it deemed to threaten its national interests. Moreover, since the mid-1970s semi-annual meetings of EC heads of state and government — what came to be called the "European Council" — introduced a top-level confederal Community "steering committee."

The ways in which EC prerogatives have expanded also reflect the Community's particular, and largely confederal, constitutional nature. The history of the European Community began with the willing co-operation of a few European nation states. Such co-operation has governed further expansions of the EC's power. Recent processes of EC constitutional change have all involved calling "intergovernmental conferences" of the EC's member states, which numbered twelve in 1992. Such conferences can be convened by a simple majority of EC members, but their conclusions must be accepted and ratified by all EC members. No treaty changes can occur without the participation and consent of all EC members.

The range of the European Community's action and "federalism" has grown of late, however. In the mid-1980s Europe responded to its grave economic problems by expanding the EC's purview and, in certain areas, changing its decision rules. The 1985 White Paper on Completing the Single Market and the subsequent Single European Act (which formally amended the founding 1957 Treaty of Rome) mandated that the Community eliminate all remaining non-tariff barriers to internal EC trade in people, capital, goods and services by January 1, 1993. The Single European Act also specified that decisions by the Council of Ministers on such matters could be reached by a "qualified majority," as opposed to earlier unanimity. In the context of the Single Market the Community was also granted new treaty bases for action in other areas such as regional development policies ("social and economic cohesion"), research and development, the environment and a limited number of social matters (largely health and safety questions). In all this the European Commission acquired a wider cluster of areas within which to make policy proposals, while the introduction of qualified majority decision making into Ministerial Council decision making began a transition from confederalism towards federalism.

The 1992 Programme succeeded beyond expectations in regenerating enthusiasm for European integration. Thus, EC members opened new negotiations in late 1990 to modify the Community's treaty base further to create an economic and monetary union (EMU). This will allow much greater economic policy co-ordination, the creation of a European Central Bank and a single currency, a very great new federalization of economic policy areas. Simultaneous negotiations on political union will expand EC jurisdiction into the fields of foreign and security policies, the regulation of immigration, drug trafficking and the control of terrorism, plus a small increase in the powers of the relatively weak European Parliament. There will also be an extension of qualified majority voting in the EC Council of Ministers.

A broad range of matters, largely economic but spilling over into strictly political realms, is now effectively regulated from EC levels and the range is likely to expand in the near future. Nonetheless, the current doctrine of "subsidiarity" states that the Community ought to acquire jurisdiction only in those policy areas that can be addressed effectively by European-level action. In general, power should be allocated to the lowest level of government appropriate for the efficient solution of specific problems. The EC's limited budgetary scope demonstrates this.

Given its provenance, therefore, EC federalism is, and will undoubtedly remain, very different from any North American varieties. The Community is an organization of "varying geometries," within which authority for different matters resides at a wide variety of different levels. "Federalized" authority in Europe is exercised in strictly delimited areas. More often, European-level decisions are made confederally, on the basis of intergovernmental consensus. Where the Community has specific constitutional competence, its laws, whether created federally or confederally, are translated into national legal codes and are enforceable through the European Court of Justice. But in those vast areas where the Community has no specified jurisdiction, national sovereignty persists unaltered.

The Community has few ambitions to "supranationalize" the identities of the citizens of Community member states. Indeed, the common tasks which member states allocate to Community action are meant to facilitate the perpetuation of those cultural distinctions which are seen as the Community's greatest strength. The Community's greatest weakness is what is commonly called its "democratic deficit." Community decisions are produced by some combination of Commission proposal and intergovernmental decision. The European Parliament has precious few powers beyond right of consultation and of amendment for certain of the measures that the Commission proposes and the Council decides. There is thus as yet no substantial Community-level legislative process to endow EC initiatives with legitimacy throughout the EC. As more and more effective power moves to Community level, this weakness is certain to become a serious problem.

Economic Union

The European Community was founded to facilitate the national and cultural survival of its member states in an era when international market developments have rendered their individual economic success problematic, if not impossible. EC poolings of sovereignty have thus far largely been in the economic area. The initial customs-free zone, common external tariff and common agricultural policy allowed EC member states and their citizens to profit greatly from post-war economic prosperity. During these years, *national* European economies profited from the economies of scale and comparative advantages allowed by vastly increased intra-Community trade.

Changed economic circumstances beginning in the 1970s revealed the limits and weaknesses of such earlier successes. Intensified globalization in the international market, the coming of new competition from Japan and the newly industrializing countries, and inflation coupled with exchange rate instability demonstrated that any given national economy within the EC was insufficient to the new tasks. This demonstration took some time, however. The later 1970s and early 1980s were a painful period of sclerosis and pessimism, when many European national economies chose self-defeating nationalist strategies out of crisis, such as promoting "national champions" in industry, non-tariff barriers in trade and beggar-their-European-neighbours macroeconomic policies.

The 1992 Single Market proposals were the response to this dark period. Behind them one can clearly see the renewal of liberalism of the 1980s. They called for *all* barriers to internal EC trade to be dismantled to transform the twelve national EC markets into a genuine single EC market where people, goods, services and capital would flow freely. Implementing this programme meant eliminating a wide range of national capacities for shaping and controlling economic life. Intra-EC border controls would no longer exist after January 1, 1993. EC member states would by then also lose the bulk of their ability to determine norms and standards, regulate banking and insurance, and decide the purchase of public goods on other than market grounds. Indirect taxation powers — VAT and excise taxes — were to be harmonized, leaving only direct taxation in the fiscal toolbox of national governments. Beyond this, the Commission has been applying EC-level competition law with increasing rigour, overseeing private sector mergers and concentrations — as Canada learned in the Dehavilland episode — making it virtually impossible for an EC member state to subsidize national industry. It has begun to dismantle state monopolies (public services) in transport and in energy (gas and electricity). Economic and monetary union will further transfer economic sovereignty away from member states, obliging EC members to harmonize their macroeconomic policies within strict limits of inflation, currency valuation, interest rate fluctuation and budget deficits. When a genuine European Central Bank and single currency are instituted, member states will have very little remaining economic policy latitude.

The 1992 and EMU processes clearly involve deregulation of European national economies, the creation of a thoroughly liberalized European single market, and the pooling and/or transfer of important parts of national economic sovereignty. The ultimate socioeconomic shape of the new European Union remains an issue of intense political struggle, however. Neo-liberals (led by the British) want to simply clear out all of the regulatory underbrush from the EC market and make Europe a free trade zone open to the winds of the international market. They hope to deregulate, depoliticize and marketize as many areas of social choice as possible, without new European regulation except to enforce free market flows. Their opponents, led by Jacques Delors and backed by the centrist Christian Democrat and Social Democrat core of European political life, want to use the revitalization and restructuring of European economic life to endow Europe with its own socioeconomic "consistency" and the capacity to act as a coherent regional pole in the international economy. These "organizers" have thus proposed programmes to accentuate what they see as a distinctive "European model of society" endowed with humane welfare state and industrial relations arrangements (the Social Charter and policies of regional "cohesion" are the centrepieces). They also advocate new-style non-*dirigiste* industrial policies to provide European firms with incentives to modernize, involving "horizontal" instruments like the promotion of research and development and the creation of European transport, telecommunications and information networks.

This struggle between neo-liberals and "organizers" is far from over. For Europe the creation of "economic union" has thus not been a value-free technical task. The desirable outlines of this economic union, rather than being regarded as self-evident, have been the object of intense debate and struggle. Progressive Europeans are quite aware that the fate of their own relatively humane capitalist societies is at stake. Beyond this, because Europe is one major location of such societies — it is not idle Eurocentric talk on the part of Jacques Delors to stress the importance of protecting and perfecting the "European model of society" — these same progressive

Europeans are conscious of participating in a conflict that is of global importance. Canada is also a relatively humane capitalist society. In Canada, as in Europe, victory by neo-liberalism in defining the logics and structures of "economic union" would be a defeat felt far beyond Canadian borders, even if Canadians would suffer most and most immediately. Thus, if there is something for Canadians to learn from Europe, beyond an understanding of the basic differences between the EC and Canadian settings, it is that what is at stake in "economic union," often disguised in plain vanilla technocratic rhetoric, is very important indeed.

Part III: Strengthening Rights

Chapter 10
Against Constitutional Property Rights

Joel Bakan

Both the common law tradition and the Québec civil code have a large place for property rights. Yet those on the right of the political spectrum want further constitutional protection for these rights. In its 1991 proposals the government undertook to entrench the right to own property in the Charter of Rights and Freedoms. Joel Bakan argues that such a measure would benefit the small minority of Canadians who own substantial property at the expense of the vast majority of Canadians. He reviews its implications for the government's ability to regulate human rights, employment, taxation, the environment and the First Nations' ability to pursue land claims. He finds that such a measure would put more power into the hands of the judiciary, which traditionally has a very conservative view of many public policy issues. In general, the constitutional protection of the right to own property could impede the pursuit of social justice.

Property rights are once again on the constitutional agenda in Canada. One wonders why, and why now. The government's explanation is not very helpful. "The

Charter does not guarantee a right to property," reads the document containing the new constitutional proposals, "it is therefore the view of the Government of Canada that the *Canadian Charter of Rights and Freedoms* should be amended to guarantee property rights." Maybe the Tories want to win back some support from the Reform Party, for whom property rights are a central plank; or maybe they want to give themselves a "bargaining chip" with which to meet proposals for a social charter of rights. Or, maybe they just cannot resist an opportunity to elevate their market ideology to constitutional status.

Constitutional property rights would serve the interests of property owners, and of these, would benefit mainly the minority of Canadians who own large amounts of property. Big business knows this — that is why they have lobbied so hard for the inclusion of property rights in the constitution. The costs of constitutional property rights would fall on the majority of Canadians who own little, if any, property, because property rights, even in the absence of constitutional protection, can be (and are) used in ways that exploit people, discriminate against them and harm the environment. Constitutional protection would serve to widen and deepen these negative effects.

In legal terms, Oxford professor A. M. Honore describes the right to property as including, first, ownership: "the 'owner' [of something] can ... use it, stop others using it, lend it, sell it or leave it by will"; and, second, "a battery of [legal] remedies in order to obtain, keep and, if necessary, get back the thing owned."[1] The right to property, in other words, means that the law will establish and protect a right to ownership of "things." A "thing" can be almost anything: personal items, real estate, money, information, stocks and bonds, to name a few. The important point is that if you have a property right in a thing, you may use that thing pretty well as you wish, exclude others from using it, and be protected by the courts in doing so. Owners of things thus have certain legally recognized powers. And if they own factories, mills, mines, apartment buildings or other kinds of commercial property, their exercise of these powers will have profound effects on workers, tenants, consumers and other members of the public, as well as on the environment.

George Bernard Shaw pointed out in 1928: "If you own an English or Scottish county you may drive the inhabitants off it into the sea if they have nowhere else to go. You may drag a sick woman with a newly born baby in her arms out of her house and dump her in the snow on the public road for no better reason than that you can make more money out of sheep and deer than out of women and men. You may prevent a waterside village from building a steamboat pier for the convenience of its trade because you think the pier would spoil the view from your bedroom window, even though you never spend more than a fortnight a year in that bedroom, and often do not come there for years together. These are not fancy examples: they are things that have been done again and again."[2]

The purpose of much modern legislative regulation is to provide at least some limited safeguards against the more egregious abuses by individuals and corporations of the power they derive from their property rights. It was apparent by the middle of this century that courts were not going to temper their enforcement of common law property rights with the recognition of competing social values, and that legislative intervention was necessary. To take one example, courts had consistently held that the common law right to property allowed owners to discriminate when employing people, doing business with them, selling or renting residences to them, or allowing them on their property. The right to property had become a licence to be racist and sexist — the law books are full of examples of how it was used in these ways.[3] According to Walter Tarnopolsky, former professor of law and now judge of the Ontario Court of Appeal, "it is no wonder ... that the legislatures, with no aid from the judiciary, had to move into the field and start to enact anti-discrimination legislation [in the 1950s and 1960s], the administration and application of which have largely been taken out of the courts."[4] Anti-discrimination law necessarily restricts common law property rights by curtailing the freedom of owners to do as they wish with their property. So do other forms of regulation designed to advance a variety of social goals, including laws relating to collective bargaining, worker health and safety, pay equity, employment standards (like minimum wages), division of marital property, landlord and tenant relations, consumer protection, broadcasting, utilities, gun control, transportation, zoning and environmental protection. Taxation (which is, of course, necessary for supporting social programmes) can also be understood as restricting property rights.

A constitutional right to property could seriously undermine the regulatory social welfare state. It would grant judges the power to decide where and when governments can regulate. A provincial or federal government could find itself being told by a court that its legislation, whether in relation to human rights, employment, taxation or the environment, violates the right to property and is thereby invalid. Big business would, of course, applaud the deregulatory thrust of a constitutional property right as a victory for "free enterprise." But for most other Canadians, whether workers, tenants, consumers or whomever, there would be little to celebrate, especially if they belong to groups historically vulnerable to the exercise of property rights — women, First Nations, people of colour, poor people, lesbians and gays, disabled people and others.

A constitutional right to property would have especially negative effects on the First Nations. It is, after all, in the name of property rights, whether those of the Crown, private corporations or individuals, that courts have excluded the First Nations from lands that are sacred to their cultures and histories, and necessary for their spiritual, social, political and economic well-being. These lands were taken by force or ceded through a treaty process in which the First Nations had little bargaining power. (The Crown has more often than not failed to live up to its minimal obligations under these treaties.) Many First Nations have made land claims, a small number of which are being negotiated.

Settlement of these claims may in some cases require governmental measures that deal with the uses and ownership structure of particular tracts of land. Such measures might be understood as limiting the property rights of current "owners" and thus running afoul of a constitutional property right. The First Nations would not be able to use the proposed constitutional right to self-government as an answer to a constitutional property right because, as in the drafted Mulroney-Clark proposals, the right to self-government is subject to the Charter, and therefore to the proposed constitutional property right. Moreover, First Nations would likely not be able to override the right to property (or any other right) through the "notwithstanding clause" because that clause applies only to Parliament and the provincial legislatures. Finally, First Nations leaders have argued that, at current rates of environmental degradation, much of the land they claim will be ruined by the time the right to self-government becomes law (the proposal recommended it not become law for ten years). A constitutional right to property may speed up the process of environmental degradation by placing a substantial obstacle in the way of environmental regulation.

Defenders of a constitutional property right argue that courts would not use the right to dismantle completely the regulatory state. That may be true, but it is equally improbable that courts would do nothing. Most likely, they would breathe enough life into a constitutional property right to threaten many existing and future regulatory régimes. Judges have always been the staunchest protectors of property rights to the point where it became necessary for legislatures to restrict common law property rights when pursuing competing social goals. Under a constitutional property right the judiciary would be handed the power to regulate the regulators in the name of a right originally of its own creation, and central to its traditions. That is a worrisome prospect.

The judiciary's application of the Charter to date highlights some of the difficulties we can expect with a Charter property right. To begin with, judges have refused to include private property owners, whether in their capacity as employers, landlords or whatever, within the scope of Charter obligations, but they have not hesitated to give them Charter protection against government regulation.[5] For example, if a shopping mall owner refuses to allow people of colour onto the premises, this will not violate the Charter. But if that same shopping centre owner runs a racist advertising campaign and the government tries to stop it, the owner can take the government to court on the ground that the government has restricted freedom of expression. This is because the Charter, even in the absence of property rights, restricts what governments can do in regulating property rights.

Justice Minister Kim Campbell (along with many others) has expressed concern about similar uses of the Charter. On the day after the government announced its 1991 constitutional proposals, she stated that judicial review under the Charter "undermines the ability of legislatures to work out public policy issues," and raises a concern that courts will "strike down progressive legislation."[6] It is unfortunate that she did not relate this concern to her government's proposal to constitutionalize property rights. For if the Charter can be a barrier to progressive legislation now, one must view with considerable anxiety an expansion of the scope of judicial review to include an explicit constitutional right to property.

Some commentators attempt to assuage the fears of property rights critics by pointing out that courts in the United States have not seriously used constitutional property rights against regulatory legislation since the 1940s. They suggest that the same approach will be taken by courts in Canada. The difficulty with this argument, however, is that it fails to account for important differences between the U.S. Bill of Rights and the Canadian Charter. Under the Bill of Rights, a regulatory limitation on the right to property is permitted so long as it is imposed with "due process." Since the 1940s, American courts have interpreted this language as requiring only that the procedures in place be fair when the government limits property rights.[7] In Canada, if the right to property is placed in section 7 of the Charter, its most likely home, any limitation will have to be consistent with the "principles of fundamental justice." Courts in Canada have interpreted this phrase as going beyond simple procedural guarantees to include the "basic tenets of the legal system,"[8] one of which is the right to property itself!

It is arguable that, despite such textual differences, the Canadian courts would respect the regulatory state in defining and applying property rights, especially with the Charter's explicit mandate that judges allow for "reasonable limits" on rights and freedoms. I am not so sanguine. When interpreting the elastic language of a constitution, courts tend to reflect the dominant ethos and mores of their time. It is therefore not surprising that the American courts, when interpreting property rights and the "due process" clause in the early part of the twentieth century, manifested a *laissez-faire* ideology. They used property rights to block introduction of the social welfare state in the 1930s, striking down minimum wage laws and other forms of progressive regulation that had been introduced by Congress and state legislatures. In the period following the Second World War, when *laissez-faire* economics had been discredited and the new economic guru was Keynes, courts shied away from their earlier approach and were more deferential towards the regulatory state. In both instances, courts were reflecting the temper of their times.

In the 1980s, not surprisingly, American courts became once again more *laissez-faire* in approach and began to revisit some of their earlier constitutional property rights ideas, to the detriment of the regulatory state. In Canada, *laissez-faire* ideology has enjoyed a renaissance under the leadership of "large C" and "small c" conservative governments beginning in the 1980s. As well, courts have taken quite an activist posture under the Charter. In these circumstances, and given the central place of property rights in the history and hearts of the judiciary, I have grave concerns about leaving it up to judges to decide what constitutes a limit on property rights, and when such limits are "reasonable."

Finally, the legal, social and political frameworks of Canada and the United States are different in ways that will substantially affect the impact of constitutional property rights. To begin with, the Canadian state has traditionally been more "interventionist" in the market than has its American counterpart. Parliament and the provincial legislatures have developed over the years a wide range of social programmes and regulation (often at the expense of private property rights) that have no parallel in the United States. Would such programmes have passed constitutional muster under the property rights guarantee in the United States? We will never know because there have been no attempts to introduce them in the United States.

Some supporters of property rights suggest that defenders of the social welfare state should not only not fear property rights, but should welcome them. Indeed, they argue that property rights may actually provide a means for protecting social rights. Benefits from the state, they point out, whether medicare, social assistance or whatever, can be understood as property entitlements and thereby fall under the protective cover of a constitutional property right. My answer: The argument is plausible in the abstract, but I don't believe that it will be accepted by the courts. Courts tend to view Charter rights and freedoms in "negative" rather than "positive" terms — as protecting individuals *from* state power, not as entitling them *to* state benefits.[9] It is difficult to see why they would alter their course under a constitutional property right. If courts are unwilling to recognize a positive dimension to equality rights, it is quite a stretch to suggest they would do so for property rights. Those who wish to see social rights protected by the constitution should spend their energies on getting explicit inclusion of such rights in the constitution, not on unrealistic and wishful thinking about property rights.

At the end of the day, constitutional property rights are a bad idea. They would empower those who are already powerful enough, at the expense of those who lack power. They would give the judiciary — an institution that has strong historical ties to property rights, and is not democratically accountable — ultimate say on the validity of regulatory decisions of democratically elected officials. Perhaps most profoundly, they would constitutionalize an ideology that is often at odds with our aspiration in Canada to build a nation that is humane, compassionate and committed to social justice.

Chapter 11

Aboriginal Peoples' Right to Self-Government

by Radha Jhappan

After centuries of injustice, the claims of native Canadians have finally become an important political issue. It remains to be seen whether the First Nations will receive constitutional recognition of their agenda. In its 1991 proposals, the government undertook to entrench in the constitution an aboriginal right to self-government which, with several limits, would be enforceable by the courts. The right would be subject to the Charter of Rights as well as to existing federal and provincial laws, and its enforceability would be delayed for up to ten years. Moreover, the government proposal failed to link self-government to the settlement of outstanding land claims. Without a base on the land, aboriginal communities may lack the economic basis for successful self-government. And the government, in its 1991 proposals, did not recognize the inherent *right to self-government. This implies that the government sees self-government as something that is within its power to grant (or withhold) from the First Nations, rather than as something that the First Nations have always possessed.*

While the 1991 proposals did not meet aboriginal constitutional demands in full, in this chapter Radha Jhappan shows that they were the most serious move towards substantive negotiations with the First Nations that any government of Canada has ever been willing to undertake.

The 1991 constitutional proposals offered by the government of Canada relating to the recognition of aboriginal peoples' right to self-government must be regarded as the most significant step forward for native political aspirations in the decade since 1982. Considering that four first ministers' conferences on aboriginal matters in the 1980s failed to produce agreement among the provinces on entrenchment of the aboriginal right to self-government, the 1991 proposals were certainly the best offer tabled to that point. Briefly, the government proposed to entrench a general right to aboriginal self-government which would be enforceable by the courts; secure a commitment from provincial governments to negotiate self-government agreements with aboriginal peoples, which are to be entrenched as they are developed; include in the constitution the requirement for a process to deal with outstanding aboriginal issues; and guarantee aboriginal representation in a reformed Senate.[1]

On the face of it, these proposals should be embraced enthusiastically by Canada's aboriginal peoples, since the first three at least would seem to satisfy the core of aboriginal groups' constitutional demands in recent years. However, the proposals in their original form raised many more questions than they answered. This is perhaps inevitable, given that their aim was to outline broad, fundamental principles, rather than to impose inflexible definitions, rules and conditions on the exercise of the rights to be entrenched. The proposals offered a skeleton of basic rights, to be fleshed out via negotiations between aboriginal peoples and the federal and provincial governments. Yet a number of vital connective tissues were missing from the proposals. This chapter thus outlines four key problems with the right to self-government as expressed in this package, before discussing the questions of inherency and the ten-year delay, the two major bones of contention to date.

Two Limits on the Right to Self-Government

Undoubtedly, a crucial source of consternation among First Nations concerns the limits which have already been placed on the right to self-government before any negotiations have begun. There are two crucial limits: first, the right would be "subject to the Charter of Rights and Freedoms"; and second, "many federal and provincial laws of general application would also continue to apply."[2]

At first sight, these limits may appear uncontroversial. In particular, it would seem reasonable to Canadians that aboriginal peoples should enjoy the rights and freedoms protected by the Charter, like any other citizens. Certainly, to the extent that the Charter protects individual and some collective rights of citizens against the actions of the federal and provincial governments, aboriginal peoples have and should continue to have the same protection as other Canadians.

However, problems may arise if the Charter is applied to the actions of aboriginal governments. It is quite possible that some of the rights enshrined in the Charter may be inconsistent with the exercise of aboriginal self-government, particularly in the case of First Nations wishing to follow their traditional forms of government within their own cultural idioms. For example, section 3 of the Charter provides that "every citizen of Canada has the right to vote in an election of ... a legislative assembly and to be qualified for membership therein." If aboriginal governments are to constitute legislative assemblies (albeit localized assemblies with limited territorial reach), what of aboriginal groups adhering to the traditions of matrilineal societies, in which political leaders (normally male) are customarily selected by women? Would an individual be able to claim that such a government was infringing on her or his democratic rights under the Charter? If so, this would thwart the operation of certain aboriginal cultural and political traditions and impose the requirement of elections according to the procedures of the dominant non-aboriginal society.

The legal rights in sections 7 to 14 of the Charter might impose similar limitations on First Nations governments committed to following aboriginal laws through tribal courts. Language, mobility and equality rights may pose other complex problems for aboriginal governments, which would not, like the federal and provincial governments, have the use of the "notwithstanding clause" to protect their laws from Charter litigation and review by the courts. Under these circumstances, the freedom of action of aboriginal governments may be seriously impeded, unless they have access to other escape clauses.

Secondly, the proposals suggested that many federal and provincial laws of general application would continue to apply to aboriginal governments. The problem here is that there are thousands of federal and provincial laws which apply to everyone within a specified territory, and of course they vary between provinces. The document did not specify which federal and provincial laws would still apply. What if fish and wildlife laws still applied? What restraints would they place on aboriginal governments' ability to manage resources, to hunt, to fish and so on? A number of aboriginal groups have clashed regularly with federal fisheries officers or provincial wildlife officers, for example, in disputes regarding the native food fishery, quotas, hunting seasons and other matters, so that depending on which general laws still apply, there could be a range of possible conflicts. At a broader level, provincial governments' control of land and resource use, particularly with respect to the leasing of lands for major resource extractive projects which affect the environment and wildlife, may clash with the interests of aboriginal governments.

The proposals did state that "the jurisdiction of aboriginal governments could potentially encompass a wide range of matters including land and resource use, language and culture, education, policing and administration of justice, health, social development, economic development and community infrastructure."[3] Presumably this would mean that the provinces would have to vacate some areas of jurisdiction, but there is no indication in the document whether aboriginal governments would have exclusive jurisdiction in some or all of these areas, or whether they will have to share jurisdictions and work out intricate arrangements through the maze of federal and provincial laws of general application. For example, it is likely that even if aboriginal governments have jurisdiction over land and resource use, this jurisdiction will be limited to their specific territories. However, the environmental and wildlife impact of provincial governments' land- and resource-use policies over the much larger territories under provincial jurisdiction will not come to a halt at political boundaries, and will undoubtedly lead to value conflicts. In that event, First Nations governments may find it difficult to persuade provincial governments to co-ordinate their land and resource policies once the jurisdictional boundaries have been drawn. In addition, as the varying needs and capabilities of different First Nations governments will necessitate different arrangements, the complexity and confusion can be expected to increase exponentially.[4]

In view of the many knotty problems engendered by the application of the Charter and federal and provincial laws, it is clear that First Nations governments must be assured that they will be able to exercise authority without being crippled by those laws. They must be given the means to exempt certain of their laws and policies from the effect of other governments' enactments. Since use of the "notwithstanding clause" by any government will be unpopular, it would probably be wiser to specify in the self-government agreements themselves (which would be constitutionally entrenched) which Charter rights are deemed not to apply to First Nations governments on the grounds of "reasonable limits."

It could be argued that First Nations governments will be protected from the relevant Charter provisions by section 25 of the Charter, which currently reads as follows:

> 25. The guarantee in this Charter of certain rights and freedoms shall not be construed so as to abrogate or derogate from any aboriginal, treaty or other rights or freedoms that pertain to the aboriginal peoples of Canada including
>
> (a) any rights or freedoms that have been recognized by the Royal Proclamation of October 7, 1763; and

(b) any rights or freedoms that may be acquired by the aboriginal peoples of Canada by way of land claims settlement.

The protection offered by this clause when it comes to the application of the Charter to aboriginal governments is open to question. Read in conjunction with section 35, which recognizes and affirms "existing aboriginal and treaty rights," it could be argued that the clause applies to the kinds of rights which have been characterized as aboriginal rights by the courts — in other words, hunting, fishing and other treaty-specific user rights. However, the right to self-government would encompass a good deal more than the user rights that can be claimed against the federal and provincial governments. As it is not clear whether the right to self-government was recognized by the Royal Proclamation of 1763, and as self-government agreements will differ qualitatively from land claims agreements, the protection offered by section 25 is not unambiguous. The courts have not interpreted its legal meaning to date. Moreover, if First Nations governments do not conform to one model, the courts will be in the position of having to apply Charter rights inconsistently according to the terms of each agreement. Finally, one must wonder what protection section 25 can offer aboriginal governments against Charter provisions, given that the government of Canada insists that the right to self-government will be "subject to the Canadian Charter of Rights and Freedoms." If this proviso is included in the clause recognizing the self-government right, it would be inconsistent with section 25.

In view of these legal problems, it would be wise for the government to clarify precisely which Charter provisions will or will not bind aboriginal governments.

Alternatively, it is possible to protect the latter from the application of certain Charter provisions, as well as from the application of certain federal and provincial laws, by including with the right to self-government a clause similar to Québec's distinct society clause. Such a clause might read as follows: "The Charter of Rights and Freedoms shall be interpreted in a manner consistent with the preservation and promotion of vibrant aboriginal communities exercising jurisdictions reached in agreements with the federal and provincial governments."

The Land Claims Question

The government's proposals of September 1991 failed to make other important connections. In particular, there was no link between the proposed self-government negotiations and land claims. The settlement of these claims, especially the comprehensive land claims of groups that have not ceded their traditional territories by treaty (approximately half the Indian population of Canada), may be crucial for their chances of successful self-government.[5] Current land bases centred on the reserves are inadequate for the economic development and resource needs of many aboriginal communities. If they are to develop economic self-sufficiency, they must be assured of a secure and expanded land base, or else resign themselves to fiscal dependency on other governments. Moreover, if the land question is not settled, we can expect accelerated jurisdictional disputes between aboriginal and provincial governments over such matters as logging and other resource-extractive projects on Crown lands licensed by the provincial governments. Yet these proposals appear to assume current land bases, and offer no suggestion that the land claims process be expedited alongside the self-government negotiations.

One of the main difficulties here will be the question of the ability of the Métis and non-status Indian peoples of Canada to exercise meaningful self-government in the absence of a land base. The proposals seem to be geared towards status Indian bands that already have a land base in the form of reserves (inadequate as they may be). Yet apart from a few settlements in Alberta and Manitoba, Métis peoples over the rest of the country do not have land bases, surely essential to the exercise of self-government.[6]

Although there are insufficient data to measure the exact size of these populations, some estimates suggest that a very rough (and very conservative) rule of thumb is that there are three Métis and non-status Indians for every registered Indian, so that the total is probably in the order of some 800 000 persons.[7] These populations, scattered across the country, are not beneficiaries of the special provisions for reserves and services under the Indian Act. This is a very important question, as Métis and non-status Indians cannot be excluded from this right, for they are identified in section 35(2) of the Charter as among the aboriginal peoples of Canada. However, the only reference to this problem in the proposals is the government's statement that it is committed to "addressing the appropriate roles and responsibilities of governments as they relate to the Métis."[8] This does not sound much like a commitment to self-government on a land base for the Métis and non-status Indian populations, yet they cannot constitutionally be excluded from the right to self-government. In the end, that right may have very little meaning for the majority of aboriginal people if the land question is not answered satisfactorily.

The Negotiation Process — Timing and Ranking

The government has proposed that in the period between 1992 and 2002 agreements can be reached in negotiations, and these would "receive constitutional protection as they are developed."[9] However, there is no indication as to which aboriginal communities would be accepted into the negotiation process, and on what basis. Is this negotiation process to be modelled after the current land claims process, wherein only six claims across the country are in negotiation at any one time, and all other groups must wait in line until the those negotiations are completed? Under this lengthy and complicated process only two agreements have been reached since 1973, and although the Council of Yukon Indians is reportedly close to a final agreement at the time of writing, that claim has taken almost twenty years to negotiate. Obviously, the government does not have unlimited personnel or resources to negotiate all claims simultaneously, and presumably this will apply to the self-government negotiations. On what basis would aboriginal groups be ranked in order to participate in negotiations? Would negotiations be between governments and bands (which were created by the Indian Act) or with wider tribal groups? Would there be a random selection, would governments decide which groups are more promising, or would aboriginal groups be asked to rank themselves? Whether the general right is entrenched in ten years or not, it is unlikely that negotiations with the 633 status Indian bands, plus numerous Métis, non-status Indian groups, and Inuit groups can be completed until well into the next century, anyway. The question of a negotiation schedule is crucial, especially because given the length of the process it might mean an asymmetrical checkerboard across the country where some aboriginal groups have constitutionally entrenched rights, while others have to wait in line.

Aboriginal Representation in a Reformed Senate

A fourth question raised by the 1991 proposals concerns Senate representation. The government of Canada noted the chronic under-representation of aboriginal peoples in federal political institutions and proposed that "aboriginal representation should be guaranteed in a reformed Senate."[10] Again, at first sight this is a laudable aim which should certainly not be rejected out of hand. However, we must wonder what difference aboriginal representation in a Senate of any form would actually make, beyond their symbolic inclusion in our national institutions. The proposal did not specify either numbers or the methods of selection or election of aboriginal representatives, so it is difficult to anticipate the desired impact. It is almost certain that aboriginal representatives would not be present in the Senate in numbers large enough to give them much political clout. The government has recommended that in matters of language and culture the Senate should have a double-majority voting rule, so that French-speaking Canadians would not be subject to the will of the non-francophone majority. However, it has not proposed a double-majority voting rule regarding matters affecting aboriginal peoples directly. Hence, it seems doubtful that aboriginal representation in the Senate will make much practical difference unless steps are taken to ensure that it is effective representation. Without a double-majority voting rule (or equivalent), it is hard to avoid the conclusion that aboriginal representation in the Senate will be little more than tokenism.

First Nations' Two Main Objections: Inherency and the Ten-Year Delay

The responses of aboriginal leaders to the government's proposals have ranged from apprehension to outright hostility. A number of leaders across the country have strongly objected to the government's failure to characterize the right to self-government as an inherent right, and the national chief of the Assembly of First Nations, Ovide Mercredi, said in late September 1991 that "if the identity of our children is of any importance to us and if we want them to stand tall and walk with pride, we have to resist, we have to reject the federal proposal."[11] Indeed, a month later, Mercredi claimed that aboriginal people could form their own government and declare sovereignty if the constitutional process fails to recognize natives' inherent rights, and insisted that aboriginal people should form a distinct society and receive treatment equal to that accorded Québec.[12]

The chief objection in the first two months after the release of the proposals revolved around the question of inherent versus legal rights. The government of Canada proposed to recognize in the Canada clause the fact that aboriginal peoples "were historically self-governing" prior to first contact with Europeans,[13] and noted that European encroachment and "a century of paternalism" under the Indian Act resulted in the erosion of their powers of self-government.[14] However, aboriginal leaders have pointed out that self-government was characterized by the government as an historical right, as an artifact, rather than as a continuing right.

In fact, aboriginal peoples have long argued that no Canadian government is in a position to grant a right which pre-dates it, a right which does not find its source in any imperial, colonial or Dominion authority. As far as aboriginal peoples are concerned, their right to govern themselves is a pre-existing, continuing, natural right given to them by the Great Creator, and it cannot be given or taken away by any government, particularly without their consent. They point out, in any case, that their right to self-government was never extinguished explicitly by treaty (which would have required their consent), nor has it been extinguished by the Royal Proclamation of 1763, or by any subsequent act of the British or Canadian governments.[15] This position has to some extent been supported by the Supreme Court of Canada in a number of important aboriginal rights decisions in recent years. Regarding treaty, hunting and fishing rights, for example, the Court has held that the Crown cannot argue that aboriginal rights have been negated by general legislation; instead, its intention to abrogate an aboriginal right must be "clear and plain."[16] Although aboriginal peoples challenge the assumption that the Crown has the power to abrogate an aboriginal right unilaterally in the first place, they can still point out that their right to self-government has never been extinguished by any "clear and plain" legislation. If they have not themselves given up the right, and if it has never been extinguished, they argue, it has survived European settlement and is not within the gift of any Canadian government.

This notion of an inherent rather than a legal right to self-government is extremely important to aboriginal people. A legal right is established by government, and thus it can be limited or revoked by government. In the 1991 proposals, the government suggested that self-government within the federation would "eliminate the need for the instruments and methods of federal intervention found in the *Indian Act*." Yet this was not a suggestion that aboriginal peoples return to their traditional forms of government in which each tribal group exercised a full range of powers appropriate to its unique needs and cultural traditions within a given territory. Rather, self-government would be a legal right enforceable by Canadian courts, and the powers and jurisdictions of each aboriginal government would be decided through negotiation with the federal and provincial governments. The right to self-government envisioned in this proposal entails authority delegated to aboriginal governments by the federal and provincial governments. Delegated authority is presumably retractable, so that aboriginal peoples may view this more as *relegated* authority, subject to the will of those governments, and lacking the protection which would be offered by the recognition of a continuing right which exists independently of those governments.

Moreover, the proposal was to entrench "a general justiciable right to aboriginal self-government," which means that the courts, as well as politicians and bureaucrats, will have a role in determining the parameters of the right. In particular, if the proposed negotiations fail to produce a definition of the right to self-government within ten years, it might be up to the courts to provide one. Aboriginal leaders object to the idea that lawyers and judges (almost without exception non-native lawyers who have little or no understanding of the needs and cultures of aboriginal peoples) might have the final word on who gets to exercise the right to self-government, where, when, how, and under what conditions and constraints. Canadian courts in the past have not taken a particularly broad view of aboriginal rights claims (with a few exceptions in the 1980s), and the increasing conservatism of the Supreme Court of Canada suggests that that Court will also take a much more limited view of aboriginal rights.[17] In such an atmosphere, aboriginal peoples are very sceptical about the prospect of giving the courts a role in the determination of their right to self-government.

This concern that the right to self-government be characterized as an inherent rather than as a legal right has more than symbolic importance for aboriginal peoples: it has real practical and political significance. The requirement that self-government agreements be negotiated with other governments, together with the role given to the courts in this proposal, would mean that more players would be involved and consequently more compromises will be necessary. Under these circumstances, aboriginal peoples' vision of their own self-governance will be much more difficult to realize.

However, while it is obvious why First Nations organizations would prefer to have an inherent right enshrined in the constitution, it is worth considering what difference the inclusion of the word *inherent* would make in real legal and constitutional terms. A strong argument can be made that the general right proposed in 1991 by the government would have as much protection as an inherent right, since it would still be the fundamental law of the land and virtually impossible to undo once enshrined. In addition, it would not be characterized merely as an historical curio, but as a right claimable in the present and in the future. Besides, even if the government were to constitutionalize the inherent right, that would still leave the division of jurisdictions, the delineation of lands and populations falling under First Nations governments, as well as practical arrangements regarding the provision of services and funding régimes to be worked out via negotiations with the federal and provincial governments.[18] It is not at all clear then that the word *inherent* would add anything substantive to the right to self-government in practical, operational terms.

However, inherency could have more serious constitutional implications beyond the practical implementation of self-government at the community level. For a long time, the government of Canada resisted the notion of the inherent right to self-government on the grounds that it could be used to support a claim to international sovereignty.[19] This is not an entirely unfounded fear, since various aboriginal groups have argued that they are sovereign nations beyond the jurisdiction of Canadian governments. For example, the Six Nations of the Iroquois Confederacy have made several dramatic declarations of independence from Canada since the 1950s, the most recent at the 1984 First Ministers' Conference on Aboriginal Matters.[20] Similarly, the Council of the Haida Nation in British Columbia declared independent nationality in 1989 (and issued passports to boot).[21] While such assertions are the exception rather than the rule in aboriginal politics, the federal and a number of provincial governments (especially Québec) can be expected to resist the constitutionalization of an inherent right to self-government if it could be construed as importing a right to sovereignty and independence from Canada.

On the other hand, all of the national aboriginal organizations have in the past made it clear that they are seeking self-government within the Canadian confederation, rather than ultimate sovereignty and independence from Canada. If this is true, then the demand for an inherent right is really a demand for a symbolic recognition of past realities and current aspirations. Such recognition might be offered by a clearer statement to that effect in either the preamble of the constitution or in the Canada clause. Therefore, First Nations organizations and leaders must decide whether casting the inherent right as the base-line demand is worth risking provincial opposition, thus scuttling the chances of negotiating real agreements which can be put into operation in the near future.

The second major source of concern is the government's proposal to delay the general enforceability of the right to self-government for up to ten years from the time the amendment is adopted. The rationale for the delay is that it will give aboriginal peoples and governments a chance to define the general nature of the right and to make sure that "the relationship between aboriginal and non-aboriginal governments is understood by all."[22] The proposal seems to suggest that the right will be entrenched at some point in the near future and then left in suspended animation for ten years. Those who object to the suspension of the right point out that Québec is not being asked to accept a promissory note, redeemable in the twenty-first century, on collective rights to preserve and promote its distinctive culture. Why, they ask, should Québec, with its history of some two hundred or so years, have its rights recognized immediately, when aboriginal peoples, whose societies in many cases have a continuous history measured in thousands of years, are asked to wait another decade?

Although this does put First Nations' needs and aspirations on hold once again, there may be sound practical reasons for delaying enforceability of the right. In the first place, the question of aboriginal rights is much more complicated, since aboriginal peoples are not concentrated within a specific province, and since the shapes and jurisdictions of aboriginal governments will vary among groups. In addition, until the thorny question of land bases (especially for currently landless groups) is settled via negotiation, entrenchment of the right to self-government will have little practical significance for many native groups. The fact is, Québec already occupies a discrete territory and exists as a province with a range of adjustable constitutional powers, whereas the creation of aboriginal governments will amount to the creation of a distinct new order of government not currently provided for in the Canadian political system.

One assumes that the government is reluctant to entrench the right to self-government now out of fear that there may be a rash of litigation as groups try to claim immediate exercise of the right when its scope has not been defined, when there are no real models already operating which can be used as guides, and when very important questions about jurisdictions, provision of services and funding have not been answered.[23] If the right were immediately included, and if certain groups availed themselves of the litigation option to speed up the process, the risk is that the courts would be charged with defining the parameters of the right, and they may not take a particularly expansive view of it. Besides — leaving aside the government's preferences — litigation (as argued above) should not be the route of choice for First Nations, since the courts are not able to settle these matters in the absence of political negotiations. If the right were immediately entrenched, at best the courts could affirm that the aboriginal litigants indeed had the said right, but they could not determine the operational details of aboriginal governments. In view of the inescapable need for negotiation, and given that agreements reached during the coming decade will be enshrined as they are developed in any case, the ten-year delay may be symbolically important, but at the practical level it may be less significant. In fact, it may well give the parties some breathing space in which solid agreements can be crafted and put into effect, without the added pressure of immediate constitutional imperatives.

For its part, the government of Québec has promised a new native policy which would entail "negotiating access to land and development rights, rather than trying to decide absolute ownership."[24] Québec's native affairs minister, Christos Sirros, has said that Québec would consider various arrangements with aboriginal people, including self-government, separate legal status and financial autonomy, to find the "proper place for natives in Québec society, somewhere between segregation and assimilation."[25] However, given the recent experiences at Oka and over the Great Whale hydroelectric project, Québec's aboriginal peoples may have little reason to trust that the government of Québec will honour their rights (not to mention the outstanding comprehensive claims to 85 percent of the lands of the province). This especially goes for the government of an independent Québec. The prospect of Québec's departure from the federation is therefore an alarming one for Québec's First Nations, whose fate may present an intractable problem for the governments concerned, even if the federal government is willing to assume its responsibilities for them. For this reason alone, aboriginal people may have a direct interest in ensuring the success of this constitutional initiative, a disconcerting consideration, to say the least.

Viewed in the context of aboriginal organizations' ultimate constitutional demands, the 1991 proposals undoubtedly fall short of the ideal. However, viewed in the context of developments in aboriginal constitutional politics over the last twenty years, the package was certainly more generous than anything offered by previous Liberal governments. The Tories' munificence can be explained by a number of factors. The Progressive Conservatives are not as committed to the individualistic, anti-communalist ideology of liberalism, which is usually hostile to claims for group rights, or for special rights accruing to groups on the basis of their ethnicity. In particular, Brian Mulroney's style of brokerage politics more easily permits accommodation of such group interests, especially where the groups concerned are politically troublesome. The fact that aboriginal peoples' exclusion from the Meech Lake process led Elijah Harper to block the accord in the Manitoba Legislature was not lost on the government. The new political prowess of aboriginal leaders must be factored into the equation now that they have shown themselves able to scuttle major initiatives which do not meet their expectations. Moreover, the effect of the Oka crisis cannot be underestimated. The increasing militancy of Indians across the country has highlighted the failure of past policies to meet the needs and aspirations of aboriginal peoples. While Oka produced a backlash against the Mohawks among some sectors of the Canadian public, submissions to the Spicer Commission as well as to the Special Joint Committee in October and November 1991 suggested a fairly high degree of support for the right to self-government for aboriginal people in general. At least, the hearings showed that many Canadians perceive a need to address aboriginal concerns through the constitution. Thus, the emergence of a generally supportive public, together with the spectre of yet another constitutional defeat at the hands of aboriginal peoples, has given the government new incentives to accommodate aboriginal demands.

Chapter 12

Women's Equality and the Constitutional Proposals

Alexandra Dobrowolsky

The women's movement has become a major force in Canadian politics, changing the way issues are addressed and putting neglected questions squarely on the public agenda. Women's equality rights are a major topic of constitutional debate. They touch almost every aspect of the government's 1991 proposals, from entrenchment of property rights in the Charter to the Charter's equality provisions. In this chapter, Alexandra Dobrowolsky points out that although women have been fighting to limit the potential for damage, men have been successful in using the Charter to the detriment of women's rights. She argues that the existing equality guarantees in the Charter must be strengthened. A feminist reading of the proposals shows that any measures that undermine the welfare state will have a particularly negative impact on women.

The Tory constitutional proposals contained in *Shaping Canada's Future Together* assume that women have achieved equality and have no further claims in the area of constitutional reform. This may be the case on purely formal grounds — with women's equality provisions in the Charter, for example. Substantively, however, pervasive and systemic inequities, discrimination and oppression are alive and well in Canada, despite the proposal's rhetoric and assurances to the contrary. As long as these conditions persist, women must — and will — continue in their struggles to change them.

Assessing the package from a feminist perspective is not a matter of singling out narrowly defined "women's issues," nor does it entail a limited focus on the Charter. Rather, a feminist analysis responds to many complex issues, from the Charter to the nature of federalism, as it addresses diverse forms of socially constructed inequality.

Equality Rights

Several of the government proposals affect women's equality rights, in particular the Canada clause and the property rights clause. In addition, the proposals fail to strengthen existing equality provisions in the Charter.

Part I of the text of the proposals sets the context for the discussion of the Canada clause. It is here that we have the first indication of the highly contentious way in which the government conceptualizes issues of gender. The document sanguinely suggests:

> Many Canadians have deep loyalties to their own communities — to a language, to a region, to an aboriginal group, to a distinct culture, to Québec as a distinct society, or to ethnic roots. We may have other ways of defining ourselves — by gender, occupation, religion or political party. But woven through all these is the sense of good for-

> tune which comes from knowing we belong to a great country, from being Canadians.[1]

This is a backhanded plea to accommodate diversity. The superficial coupling of gender with other categories such as occupation, religion and political party shows a lack of appreciation of what gender is all about. Gender is about power relations, about how society is stratified so that men have power over women; it is about how women's lives are historically constructed and currently organized; and it is about how women interact in their individual relationships and in their communities. This is not to say that gender is not linked to occupation (class), religion (discrimination based on religion and within religions) and political party (under-representation of women), but rather that this is a superficial categorization, which denies these complex relations and serves to devalue the realities of women.

The Canada clause itself is problematic for what it includes and for what it excludes, and for the presumptions and assumptions it makes. It haphazardly mentions equality between women and men, discusses fairness and full participation of people without regard to race, colour, creed, physical or mental disability or cultural background, recognizes aboriginal peoples, designates Québec a distinct society, discusses sustainable development, the well-being of Canadians ... and the list continues. It appears that the government is trying to cover all its bases with this section, and yet it has failed to do so. If the government is trying to please everyone, why not mention discrimination on the basis of sexual orientation, or age? The government's document makes a shopping list of these various inequities without either comprehending their interconnection or taking their ramifications seriously.

Paradoxically, many of the principles listed in the Canada clause are contradicted in the provisions that follow. For instance, the "well-being" of Canadians will be in question because of the proposals' off-loading of many federal powers onto the provinces, which may lead the way to inconsistent standards of care across the country. Further, the creation of new programmes will be difficult. As just one example, it is highly unlikely that "well-being" will encompass free, accessible abortion services for women. Therefore, despite the government's rhetoric in the Canada clause, there are discrepancies between what it says and what it then proposes to do.

Finally, the Canada clause affirms "equality between women and men," the assumption being that this equality already exists. The danger here is that such a statement may make it appear that women are no longer disadvantaged. If this is the case, this may, for example, detract from section 16(2) of the Charter which supports affirmative action for women. Indeed, if equality is presumed, then the government can forestall action on employment equity or other measures that try to redress lived inequalities between women and men.

With respect to the incorporation of property rights, it is clear that the federal government is once again under the misconception that women have achieved equality. This is the only explanation for the government's insensitivity to the fact that women will be negatively affected by a property rights provision. First, because women are poorer than men, women do not have the same access to, or capacity to acquire, property that men do. In Canada, in 1987, full-time working women's earnings were 66 percent those of men.[2] To be sure, this rate of income also varies among women. Aboriginal women's total income median is just under three-quarters that of their non-aboriginal counterparts.[3] Women with disabilities are consistently unemployed or underemployed, which translates into minimal income levels.[4] The growing feminization of poverty means that the idea of equal access to property is more formal than real.

There are a number of other dangers. For instance, there is the risk that property rights may chip away at gains made by women in terms of family law reform and division of spousal property in divorce; that is, the property rights provision could open the way for claims that property-sharing laws are unconstitutional. Moreover, native women may take issue with property rights that could conceivably take precedence over the collective rights of aboriginal peoples to their ancestral lands. The entrenchment of property rights may even open the field for discrimination in terms of rents, tenancy and housing. Women are more likely than men to be subject to these problems, for fewer women possess their own homes: in 1986, only 42 percent of female heads of households were likely to own their homes in contrast to 70 percent of male heads of households.[5] Discrimination on the basis of sexual orientation commonly occurs in housing. The invocation of property rights may give another justification for such discriminatory practices. And lastly, equal pay for work of equal value may come under scrutiny as employers may defend their right to allocate revenues as they deem appropriate. In sum, by promoting property rights, the government is sanctioning and entrenching unequal power relations.

Rather than undermining the few gains that women have achieved, the government should take this opportunity to strengthen the equality sections in the Charter. This is the position taken by the National Action Committee on the Status of Women (NAC).[6] Moreover, one might consider NAC's call for stronger wording in section 28 as a way of allaying any fears, lingering from the Meech Lake process, regarding the potential of the distinct society clause to detract from women's equality rights inside Québec. In its brief, NAC has made its support of the distinct society clause very clear, but it also has suggested that the concern "should not be with the distinct society clause, but rather with the weakness of the wording of Section 28 on the equality of women."[7]

Canada's equality guarantees have been in effect for over half a decade.[8] Unfortunately, studies have shown not only that women's use of the Charter has been limited, but also that men have used the Charter's equality provisions and others to restrict laws that benefit and protect women.[9] Men have turned to equality guarantees three times as often as women. They are also more likely to use these provisions to defend themselves from criminal prosecution than to seek distributive justice. For instance, in the area of criminal law, men have tended to employ equality provisions to challenge sexual assault laws. The recent striking down of the rape shield law is one example of men's use of certain sections of the Charter (beyond equality provisions) to the detriment of women. Ironically, women's groups are now having to work to reduce the damage potential of the Charter. This record casts doubt on the measure of women's equality in Canada. It also makes an argument for strengthening sections 15 and 28, at the very least, and perhaps more ambitiously for establishing some form of a social charter, as proposed by the Rae government in Ontario.[10]

Institutional Reforms

In spite of the gradual increase in the number of women in politics, there are still relatively few women sitting in

Parliament and the provincial legislatures.[11] In the House of Commons, for example, only 13 percent of the total members are women, while in the Senate they are 12 percent.[12] Women therefore lack the opportunity to voice their experiences of the world. As well, there is a marked under-representation of people of colour and aboriginal peoples. Because their numbers are few at decision-making levels, women and these other groups continue to find themselves reacting to proposals that are drafted and policies that are made without their concerns in mind.

Institutional reforms have the potential to tackle these problems and to make Canada into a true representative democracy. *Shaping Canada's Future Together* took almost no initiative in this respect.

The document called for two major institutional changes: reform of the Senate and the establishment of a Council of Federation. It endorsed an elected and equitable Senate, with guaranteed representation for aboriginal peoples. The meaning of "equitable" is unclear, although some women's groups argue that steps towards ameliorating women's political under-representation can be taken if half the Senate seats are reserved for women and others who lack representation in our system.

The proposal for a new institution, the Council of Federation, is problematic in that the Council would create a third level of government composed of ministerial representatives from the federal and provincial governments (territorial representatives would participate as non-voting members) which would function along the lines of a permanent federal-provincial conference. It would be unelected, and so raises questions about accountability as well as representation. This is reminiscent of the predominately male, executive level of networking which brought us the Meech Lake Accord. Indeed, the Council of Federation can be deemed a method of institutionalizing the same type of executive federalism which prevailed with Meech Lake. Given women's exclusion from that process, they have every reason to be worried about the proposed Council of Federation.

There are also a number of minor reforms projected in the document. For example, the proposals indicated that there would be a loosening of party discipline and more rein for free votes, but this means little to women if they still lack representation. The pressure placed on Tory MPs to support the government's abortion legislation, a supposedly "free vote," highlights the gap between theory and practice in this realm.

If the government has put these major and minor reforms on the table, then why does it refrain from adopting structural changes that may truly favour women, people of colour, natives and others who presently lack numbers in the supposedly representative and democratic system? For example, mounting evidence establishes that proportional representation gives women a better chance of being elected. Or, more radically, recommendations have been made to adopt dual member, rather than single member, constituencies where both a woman and a man are elected for each riding. The government's institutional reforms coincide with both its decentralist strategies and its executive federalist tendencies. They do not regard substantive changes which have the capacity to begin to redress current representational inequalities.

Decentralization and the Neo-Conservative Agenda

Finally, of central importance to women is the whole decentralist tone of the proposals, from their transfer of labour-market training to the provinces to their potential to back away from shared-cost programmes. Devolution of federal powers is apparent on many levels. Beyond labour-market training, Ottawa would transfer to the provinces all matters not specifically assigned to the federal government under the constitution or by virtue of court decision; it would recognize exclusive provincial jurisdiction in tourism, forestry, mining, recreation, housing and municipal affairs; and the proposals list a host of candidates for "streamlining," from wildlife protection and soil and water conservation, to some aspects of financial sector regulation and unfair trade practices.

The most alarming decentralizing tendency is apparent in the spending power provision. Any new federal spending in the areas of provincial jurisdiction requires the agreement of seven provinces with 50 percent of the country's population. However, provinces can opt out with compensation if their own programmes meet federal objectives. The concept of "meeting objectives" seems to be weaker than the wording in Meech, which stipulated that provincial programmes had to be "compatible with" national objectives. The devolution of federal powers and the spending power allowances do not bode well for social programmes. They come as little surprise, however, for they fit with the neo-conservative agenda the Mulroney government has followed over the past, which has favoured transfers to business over spending on social programmes.[13]

The decentralization advocated in the proposals would affect women in a variety of ways. First, inconsistent standards of care have an acute impact on women, for they, more than men, depend on programmes like medicare, extended health care, social assistance, old age assistance and child care. Women bear children and have been culturally assigned the responsibility of child-rearing and caring for the sick, the old and others. Moreover, women predominate among the elderly poor. If basic uniform standards of care are not met, women will bear the brunt of the inadequacies. Second, decentralization puts into question the establishment of new national programmes such as day care. Third, devolution of federal powers could conceivably mean more lobbying work for women in pursuit of their rights; women will have to mount campaigns on provincial fronts as well as the national front. This may also detract from the power of national women's groups and the ability for women from across the country to unite and mobilize.

There are numerous concrete reasons for women to challenge the federal government's 1991 constitutional proposals. Women's concerns are not limited to single issues or Charter references. The government must be made aware of its continued exclusion of women, its misconceptions surrounding equality, and its lack of understanding regarding "women's issues," gender and feminist analysis. It is of the utmost importance for women to make their objections known to the government, and to make it clear that they deserve and require more substantive consideration. It is imperative that this dissent be voiced, for it may be a long while before women have another such opportunity to affect the process of constitutional change.

Chapter 13

The Social Charter

David P. Shugarman

As a member of the United Nations, Canada has accepted international treaty obligations to promote social and economic rights. No similar commitment exists in the constitution.

The idea of a social charter that would complement the existing Charter of Rights and Freedoms has been put forward by Audrey McLaughlin and Ontario Premier Bob Rae. In this chapter, David P. Shugarman reviews what this would entail. He sees rights as entitlements necessary to the democratic process. As opposed to property rights, which exclude people, economic and social rights are rights of inclusion that enhance personal development and social well-being. There are various options available for promoting social rights, including amending the existing Charter so as to include basic rights to a clean environment and economic and social security, rights Canada has already accepted internationally.

On February 13, 1992, Premier Bob Rae released a statement entitled *Ontario's Proposal for a Social Charter*. The statement "proposes that the social charter be entrenched in section 36 of the Constitution Act, 1982, and that it speak in terms of the commitment of governments to meet social policy objectives." The statement goes on to list five commitments that are to be added to section 36(1). The commitments are to medicare; programmes providing minimum levels of housing, food and other basic necessities; high-quality public primary and secondary school education; maintaining and improving the quality of the environment; and improving "the quality and standard of life of Canadians." Furthermore, the Ontario proposal sought to remedy the legal impotence of section 36 by calling for intergovernmental agreements covering the social charter to be constitutionally binding (i.e. presumably subject to review by the courts). There are further proposals which deal with implementing and monitoring the social charter, harmonizing it with the Charter of Rights and Freedoms and making federal-provincial agreements on national standards "less restrictive."

Two weeks later, the Parliamentary Special Joint Committee on a Renewed Canada (also known as the Beaudoin-Dobbie Committee) issued a report containing approximately sixty recommendations. Included in the recommendations is a call for a "new social contract among Canadians." This amounts to an endorsement of a social charter that, with a few notable exceptions, is very similar to the Ontario proposal. The Committee did not endorse Rae's suggestion for making governmental agreements binding. However, there are proposals for a new section 95 of the Constitution Act, 1982 which would address some of Rae's concerns. The Committee did adopt Rae's declarations of commitments, softening the language somewhat, and adding in the right of workers to organize and bargain collectively (the only mention of "right" in the commitments, and a concern curiously omitted in the proposals of an NDP government). The Joint Committee recommends that the new social contract should be constitutionally entrenched as the Canadian Social Covenant.

The Purpose of a Social Charter

In one sense the purpose of a social charter is to catalogue and protect various claims, entitlements and powers that are often referred to as economic and social rights. Advocates of economic and social rights see them as intrinsic goods which are integral to a thoroughgoing democracy and essential to the development of a co-operative and caring political community. In this regard social justice is nothing less than the exercise and satisfaction of these rights.

This proposition on its own provides the grounds for bringing such rights into our constitution. Furthermore, social charter proponents point to the significance of Canada's affirmative vote on the 1977 UN General Assembly Resolution 32/130 which states not only that "all human rights are indivisible and interdependent," but also that "the full realization of civil and political rights without the enjoyment of economic, social, and cultural rights is impossible."

There is another compelling reason for extending our constitutional rights. Given the present context of colliding sensibilities and rival interpretations of Canadian history as well as current political intentions, a shared commitment to establishing positive economic and social rights could be a new source of national unity. This might be a way of transcending differences over changes in the federal division of powers (even perhaps the changes encompassed in versions of asymmetrical federalism). In a related manner, it can be argued that the exercise and expression of these rights would be reflective of the shared values, collective sense of identity and aspirations of Canadians.

There are some political leaders, commentators and constitutional authorities who continue to believe that the adoption of the Charter of Rights and Freedoms was a regressive step in Canada's constitutional development. This belief, expressed sometimes by those on the political left and sometimes by those on the right, reflects a fear and perception that orientation to rights is somehow so legalistic, so individualistic and so American that community sensibilities and priorities are undermined at the same time that lawyers and judges usurp the functions of representative legislatures. Such a belief stems from a highly attenuated notion of the nature of rights that dates back to seventeenth-century English natural rights theorists, a notion Canadian political philosopher C. B. Macpherson identified as the possessive individualist strain in early modern liberalism.[1]

There is, however, a more expansive appreciation of the role and nature of rights, one that is more compatible with the principles of a modern liberal democracy. In this appreciation, rights are derived from the assumption that in order to develop one's personality as a free human being in association with others a person must be entitled to participate in and partake of the common wealth or the community well-being.

This understanding of rights also fits in with the notion that constitutions are more than designations of powers and authority, or specified constraints on governors and governed. Constitutions are constitutive of collective identity and collective practices. Constitutional rules and regulations are not necessarily restrictive; they are also facilitative. They may facilitate personal development and collective action. Constitutional rights in the expansive and developmental sense are conducive to enhanced citizenship and empowerment.

Some critics contend that entrenching rights and fostering rights consciousness will divide, mystify and demobilize the disadvantaged. The irony here is that this contention ignores the fact that demands for the recognition and expansion of political, economic and social rights are reflective of democratic movements to build a more co-operative and more sharing society. Traditionalists are anxious about rights precisely because they understand all too well that the demand for rights is a threat to the privileged and powerful. In his *Reflections on the French Revolution*, Edmund Burke put the conservative case against the expansion of rights starkly: "The more the objects of ambition are multiplied and become democratic, just in that proportion the rich are endangered."[2]

In a democratic age no politician campaigning for election would dare be as blunt as Burke. Instead the modern Burkean will warn of the dangers of encouraging expectations which he believes are so abstract and utopian that they can never be met, of relying on judges instead of trusted political leaders, of overburdening governments, and of the high cost and inefficiencies associated with social welfare programmes, and the inappropriateness of mandating public intervention in areas best left to market determination and private initiative. Paradoxically, the case *for* establishing positive economic and social rights is reliant on the strength of the opposition to them. In this regard, arguments about rights are not abstract but quintessentially political: they are about equality and power.

Much of the impetus for placing a social charter on the constitutional agenda came from recommendations put forward in the summer and fall of 1991 by federal

NDP leader Audrey McLaughlin and Ontario Premier Bob Rae. McLaughlin and Rae's initiatives found a receptive audience and were quickly supported and supplemented by a number of Canadian organizations, equality rights groups and social movements (such as the Canadian Centre for Policy Alternatives, the Canadian Council on Social Development, the National Anti-Poverty Organization and the Centre for Equality Rights in Accommodation). In October 1991, the Environics polling firm reported survey data indicating that 85 percent of Canadians (and a slightly higher proportion in Québec) were in favour of "a social charter that would guarantee the right to health care, social assistance and education." In retrospect it seems clear that both McLaughlin and Rae were sensitive to emerging contradictions and a possible collision between our changing political culture and a changing political economy. An understanding of this political context is crucial to an appreciation of the generation and development of the social charter idea.

A Changing Political Culture

What we have been witnessing over the past decade is the development of an increasingly egalitarian and democratic political culture. The much-remarked Canadian disposition to defer to political élites and customary processes of decision making has been replaced by distrust of traditional political leaders, antipathy for traditional political manoeuvrings and cynicism about the virtues of parliamentary government. Scrutiny of leaders and demands for empowerment are now valued more highly than deal making among élites.

Our political culture is also being transformed in other ways. Canada is being transformed by multiculturalism both demographically and politically. Together with increasing sympathy for increasingly activist aboriginal groups, multiculturalism has meant that for many people a definition of Canada as an alliance of two nations or two founding peoples is unacceptable. The notion that we are defined in terms of a unique English-French accommodation tied together by an east-west economy has dissipated.

Being Canadian is coming to be associated with institutionalized measures and norms that are regarded as protecting and enhancing our quality of life. Medicare and the Charter have become new sources of pride and patriotism. They may be well on the way to becoming recognized Canadian birthrights.

Since its adoption in 1982, the Charter has become an important national symbol all across anglophone Canada. It is worth noting that just prior to the conflict over the Meech Lake Accord, Canadians both inside and outside Québec spoke of the Charter in nearly motherhood terms. In a survey conducted at York University, three-quarters of French Canadians living in Québec indicated some familiarity with the Charter. Of those, 98 percent said that the Charter was a good thing rather than a bad thing for Canada. In the rest of Canada, 89 percent of those asked claimed they had heard of the Charter and 92 percent of them held that the Charter was a good thing for the country. These data should not be surprising since the Charter legitimized the interests of a majority of Canadians who had been largely excluded from the earlier constitutional agenda. And in Québec it is reasonable to assume that the province's own Charter of Rights reinforced a positive disposition to rights documents.

For aboriginals, women, the disabled, visible minorities, ethnic and religious minorities and others, the

Charter has supported the assertion of individual and group rights and encouraged participation in constitutional discourse. Where constitutional issues in the past had largely been jurisdictional disputes between governments, the Charter now focuses on relationships between governments and citizens. The concept of citizenship has been enhanced. The scope of citizen activity has been expanded.

Our transformed political culture is very much a Charter culture. The Charter has created an environment of rights consciousness and contributed to a sense of citizen empowerment. It has engendered a feeling that as Canadians we all share and enjoy fundamental freedoms, that we now have a constitution *that speaks for us,* and that it is *our* constitution. The expression of these new sensibilities instils "Charter patriotism." The changing nature of Canada means that there is a receptive climate for strengthening rights. Yet this optimistic orientation to rights in a democratizing political culture has run up against conservative Charter jurisprudence and neo-conservative political economics.

The Social Charter and the Charter of Rights and Freedoms

The Charter replaced the common law and legislative supremacy ideological tradition by explicitly casting a constitutional sanction of rights within a democratic orientation to social values.[3] If we understand the Charter as a *democratic* bill of rights, then rights are not to be understood as possessions that are somehow prior to and to some extent antagonistic to democracy — this is an orientation that goes back to the natural rights theories of the seventeenth century and figures prominently in American jurisprudence — but are, rather, accepted as entitlements necessary to the democratic process.

In numerous judgements the Supreme Court of Canada has underscored the democratic purpose of both the Charter and the judicial review function. In *Morgentaler v. the Queen,* former chief justice Brian Dickson summarized this perspective in stating that "Canadian courts are charged with the crucial obligation of ensuring that the legislative initiatives pursued by our Parliament and legislatures conform to the democratic values expressed in the Canadian Charter." And in an earlier case, *R. v. Oakes,* the chief justice stated that "the values and principles essential to a free and democratic society" include "commitment to social justice and equality" and "social and political institutions which enhance the participation of individuals and groups in society." Such remarks — when set alongside Charter references to a democratic society in section 1 and to equality rights in section 15, and taken together with the obligation, set out in Part III section 36 of the Constitution Act, 1982, to promote equal opportunities and economic development "for the well-being of Canadians" and to provide "essential public services of reasonable quality to all" — would seem to suggest that we already have constitutionalized economic and social rights.

Unfortunately, in this respect the Charter has been a source of frustration and disappointment. The courts have been inclined to treat economic and social rights as policy matters determinable by particular legislatures rather than as fundamental. So they are regarded as undeserving of Charter protection.

This is especially the case with workers' rights. Over the eloquent objections of the former chief justice and former justice Bertha Wilson, the Supreme Court decided that collective bargaining and striking, which are essential activities of trade unions, are not Charter rights. In other decisions the Court has held that lawful picketing is an activity protected by the Charter, but that picketing courthouses is unlawful. What is doubly troubling about the Court's deference to legislatures on the matter of the scope and substance of social and economic rights is that it has coincided with calls and measures (by certain interest groups and particular governments) to systematically reduce national social programmes and either restrict or privatize the provisions of goods and services. This is a neo-conservative agenda that mocks the intent of section 36.

Confronting Neo-conservatism

Over the past twenty years the political climate has not been conducive to improvements in social welfare. Much has been made of government deficits, social expenditures and the inefficiencies of the welfare system. During this period we have seen provincial and federal governments legislate wage and price controls, the "6 and 5" programme, back-to-work legislation, and restrictions on trade union freedoms. Recessionary periods over the past two decades have increased the numbers of the unemployed, the homeless and people generally dependent on federal and provincial insurance and assistance plans. The so-called crisis of the welfare state has occurred because some business leaders and governments have questioned the cost, cost-effectiveness and ideological propriety of an expanding welfare system and are intent on reducing or eliminating those aspects of it which they find unproductive and/or threatening.

However, the evidence from recent major studies of public opinion indicates clearly that in Western Europe and North America most people are not disposed to dismantling or reducing established social security provisions and measures. In a recent edition of *How Ottawa Spends*, Seymour Wilson notes that "all public opinion survey data indicate that the public is not prepared to make deep cuts or cancel government social programs."[4]

There is little evidence that Canadians consider government action in the provision of social welfare somehow less legitimate now. On the contrary, many Canadians are concerned that governments intent on fiscal restraint may loosen their commitment to ameliorate the living conditions of the disadvantaged and to prevent their being deprived of subsistence, security and participation. They are also concerned about the maintenance of universally accessible and equitable health care, which has become both an essential public service and an overwhelmingly shared national value. What people are learning is that when rights are not guaranteed, when they are not deemed as fundamental within the constitutional sphere, they come to resemble permissions that are subject to denial by a resolutely ideological government or one that puts expediency before principle. That is why so many people now believe that it is necessary to bring what we have been calling economic and social rights into the constitution.

When Social Rights Are Economic Rights

There is a redundancy involved in speaking of economic *and* social rights. In a sense, all rights are social (no matter whether we treat them specifically as individual or collective, positive or negative, moral or legal, primary or secondary). When someone has a right to do or use something, it means — as John Stuart Mill pointed out 130 years ago — that a sufficient claim has been societally legitimated so that the individual is guaranteed that thing by society. When a right to (for example) publicly administered hospital and medical care is constitutionally entrenched, the fundamental law of the country is understood to protect and advance the interests of all Canadians on the assumption that provision of these benefits and services is a good for every Canadian; and furthermore, that it is a good so essential that the constitution implies that it is illegal to deprive citizens of it. Following Mill, to show that a person's claim to have a right to something is invalid is to demonstrate "that society ought not to take measures for securing it to him, but should leave him to chance, or to his own exertions."[5] So, neither the determination of a right nor its denial rests with the individual. In both cases the onus is on society, which must advance arguments (philosophical, legal and political) as to what interests are to be protected and advanced by society and how.

Economic-social rights can perhaps best be understood as rights of inclusion (in contrast to traditional property rights, which are rights to exclude). These are rights to develop one's personal attributes in co-operation with others and to have a relatively equal share of the resources and benefits of society, whatever one's capacities. It is sometimes thought that this species of rights is categorially and logically distinct from legal and political rights. The alleged distinction conceives of the latter as negative in nature and exercise, in the sense that the existence of the right negates interference from others (including the state), while it conceives of economic-social rights as positive, in the sense that others (including state institutions) are required (duty-bound) to do something to facilitate the exercise of the right.

A moment's reflection on a few examples indicates that the distinction is deceptively simple and misleading. Consider two of the legal rights that are specified in section 11 of the Charter of Rights: the right to be presumed innocent until proven guilty in a fair and public trial before an independent and impartial tribunal, and the right to be tried by a jury. Inasmuch as these are procedural safeguards that block the state from violating one's physical security they may be construed as classic negative rights. But it is also clear that for these rights to be effectively exercised many other people are duty-bound to do certain things and the state is obligated to spend a good deal of money. These are rights that quite clearly require the collective actions of others whose rights are not being claimed.

Now consider the so-called positive economic rights to collective bargaining and striking (which were not specifically included in the Charter). These are positive in the double sense that they call for specific lawful responses by another party (the employer) and that such actions clearly impinge on the actions and liberties of that other party. But these rights also have a decidedly negative aspect: if and when they are exercised, the state is required not to take sides and not to intervene in a lawful negotiation-and-dispute process.

The traditional argument that usually attends this alleged categorial distinction is that since economic and social rights are positive and thus more complex, more cumbersome, more invasive and more expensive than civil and political rights, the former should be treated as secondary. Therefore, it is argued, the entrenchment of positive social rights should be addressed cautiously and their justiciability (their ability to be enforced by the courts) recognized as problematic. However, once we see that the distinction between positive and negative rights is far from neat, the elaborate argument that rests on the distinction and which is used to deny the fundamental importance of social rights collapses.[6]

Furthermore, if we are willing to grant that a minimal level of economic security is at least as important to personal development and the enjoyment of life as physical security — in fact, serious deficiencies in essentials such as uncontaminated water, nutritious food and adequate shelter amount to denial of physical security — then we need to recognize the right to a basic level of economic security as a fundamental right and a core value around which are clustered related rights.[7] More specifically (and not exhaustively), they are rights to clean air, potable water and uncontaminated food; to a decent standard of living and the protection and, whenever possible, improvement of humane, safe accommodation and working conditions; to participation in collective action and decisions affecting one's working life, including organizing, bargaining and striking; to rest and recreation; to paid maternity and paternity leave; to economic and social security including universal medical and dental care, child care and legal aid.

Most of these items have been adapted from the International Covenant on Economic, Social and Cultural Rights. Some can be found in other documents that make up the International Bill of Rights. Many of these rights could be accommodated by adding subsections to sections 2 and 15 of the Charter. Canada has signed and ratified these international covenants along with over sixty-five other nations; their provisions are not the fanciful creations of beings from another planet, whatever conservatives and neo-conservatives may say. The problem is that these rights are for the most part not exercised in this country. Like the implied promise of economic and social rights in the Constitution Act, 1982, they remain as rhetoric, not reality.

Options for Realizing Our Rights

As has been pointed out, Canadians are concerned to protect and improve our social security programmes and medicare. It is to be expected that they will be receptive to measures that secure these benefits as economic-social rights, but it is not clear what the most appropriate measures are. The options presented in the following are by no means all mutually exclusive.

1. Adopt the approach of international lawyers who argue that Canada should make good on its commitments to international covenants; they would lobby legislators and educate judges to draw on these agreements as sources for the interpretation of the Charter. From this perspective Canada is part of an evolving network of international law. Lawyers in Britain have recently had some success following this route. They have taken before the European Court of Human Rights several cases of governmental abuse of rights guaranteed by the European Convention on Human Rights. The trouble with this option is that it leaves the pursuit of rights and redress solely in the hands of specialists in international law.

2. Entrench a set of declaratory principles oriented to the protection of highly cherished social programs and shared values. This might provide a political and moral restraint on governments, though there would be no constitutional basis for enforcement. The difficulty with this tack is that it invites cynicism ("much ado about nothing"). The trouble with dressing up commitments to a social charter by placing them in a preamble to the constitution or by proclaiming them as constitutional

commitments of governments is that this neglects the important substantive legal principle *Ubi ius ibi remedium* — where there is a right there is a remedy. A non-justiciable approach turns attention away from citizens as rights claimants and agents. It focuses on governments' goals and on agreements among governments to safeguard and promote policies and programs in their subjects' interests. This is not very far removed from the third option, a very traditional one.

3. Leave the protection of rights to various legislatures. This traditionalist alternative appeals to those who distrust the courts and are worried about unelected judges making political policy. The traditionalists have promoted a good deal of confusion over the nature of rights, rights adjudication and political decision making. While they hold that these activities are practically indistinguishable, they also, curiously, hold that law and politics are worlds apart and should remain so. What they fail to understand is that it is up to Canadians and their elected representatives to determine what rights should be designated as fundamental and constitutionally protected. It is up to legislatures to devise policies and programs consistent with these guarantees. And it is up to the courts to determine if and why our rights are being infringed or denied. There are serious practical drawbacks to the traditional approach. Given the existence of the Charter of Rights, a legislative bill of economic-social rights would probably receive less notice from both the courts and legislatures than the Diefenbaker Bill of Rights. Moreover, as mentioned earlier, when the determination of rights is left to the whims of interest groups and brokerage politics we leave the domain of rights and return to the traditional realms of permission and benevolence.

4. Constitutionalize a charter of economic and social rights. This would follow the example of the United Nations or the system of reporting and supervision associated with the European Social Charter. Having passed the Universal Declaration of Human Rights, the UN then proceeded to draft two separate though by no means contradictory or mutually exclusive covenants on rights, one covering civil and political rights and the other treating economic, social and cultural matters. The latter covenant has a general "promotional" approach to its rights and it emphasizes the value of "progressive implementation." The strategy followed to bring in economic and social rights and the substantive thrust of the covenant may be worth emulating, especially if there is sustained resistance to expanding the provisions of the Charter of Rights. However the International Covenant lacks any enforcement procedures. States are expected to report on their own progress. There is no mechanism of protest available for those whose rights have been denied. The problem with the principle of progressive implementation is that it provides governments with a built-in rationale for procrastination: "In principle we're committed to the principle of progressive implementation but we still have to make progress on the question of how to implement ... " And it accepts the secondary ranking of economic-social rights.

The European Social Charter, adopted by the Council of Europe in 1961, may be viewed as a more attractive non-justiciable model for rights protection. The European Charter lists nineteen rights for potential protection, sets out requirements for implementation and includes a three-stage reporting and supervision procedure. Participating states are required to adopt five of seven "essential" rights and at least five others. Every two years, states are required to report on the nature of their compliance with the Charter's provisions. The reports are then reviewed by a committee of experts. This committee then sends the reports and their reviews to an intergovernmental committee that can issue recommendations regarding a state's compliance. In contrast to the International Covenant, the European Charter does have a partial enforcement mechanism, but it is one that is administrative rather than judicial and binding.

5. Trust progressive lawyers and judges to appreciate the democratic nature of the Charter and incrementally build a new tradition devoted to the defence and expansion of democratic liberties. Canadians and Canadian lawyers will become more familiar with the Charter. If in doing so they become more amenable to the notion of rights that are fundamental to democracy, then it is to be expected that our future judicial authorities will jettison the decidedly undemocratic tradition of our earlier constitutional régime. This is a big "if" and it is something that won't happen overnight. Optimism that this scenario will come about is not an argument for leaving the struggle for democratic rights to lawyers and judges. The legal route is complex and expensive (which is another argument for a universal legal plan) and no substitute for the creativity of responsible politicians. Nevertheless, it would be a mistake to assume that the way to build a democratic political community and advance citizens' interests is an either/or proposition: the legislature or the courts; the law or the home, office and factory; parliamentary parties or extraparliamentary movements. While it is no panacea for social problems, entrenching social rights in the constitution and relying on the courts as guardians of the constitution will be important in achieving these goals. These considerations lead us to the next and best option.

6. Amend the Charter of Rights so that it incorporates economic-social rights and strengthens and supplements provisions guaranteeing equality and committing governments to equalization across Canada. In the early stages of the process of constitutional renewal there were reasons to doubt the appropriateness of this approach with respect to achieving a resolution of the crisis in Canadian federalism: first, because it could be construed by Québecers and aboriginal peoples as avoiding or subordinating their concerns about the division of federal powers and the protection of their distinct societies; and second, because opening the Charter up for revision ran the risk of putting everything up for grabs and dropping economic-social rights to a low priority amidst the inevitable shuffle to add, revise and redefine.

As the constitutional process evolved, however, it became apparent that there was widespread, grass roots support for a constitutionally binding, justiciable approach to rights protection. The government of the largest province in Canada had put economic-social rights on the political agenda as a matter of high priority. The negotiation process over Canada's future was for a time largely taken up with cost-benefit projections by accountants masquerading as political economists on the one hand and by claims about the importance of ethnic nationalism on the other. The social charter debate has engendered discussion of what it means to be a citizen of Canada and how membership in this particular country provides us with opportunities for personal development and social well-being — no matter where we live or which of the official languages we use. Rights talk and rights claims — rights consciousness — are legitimate demands of people who want to develop their powers as sociable individuals and who "know and value what it means to participate in and be responsible for the care and improvement of a common and collective life."[8]

The Beaudoin-Dobbie Social Covenant

The recommendation of a social covenant by the Beaudoin-Dobbie Committee, which generally follows Premier Rae's mid-February proposals, resembled the second option outlined above. With respect to the enunciation and constitutional protection of rights, it is the least substantive of all the options considered. Beaudoin-Dobbie would rewrite Part III, section 36 of the Constitution Act, 1982. That section is not part of the Charter of Rights. It deals with governmental commitments to economic and social goals, not citizens' rights. As the Beaudoin-Dobbie Committee acknowledges, the amendments they proposed to section 36 would continue to be commitments to goals, not to rights. And while the report borrowed from the model of the European Social Charter by calling for compliance to be reviewed through public hearings and periodic reports by an intergovernmental agency, it would still be left to individual governments and legislatures — and ultimately (and ideally) the electorate — to decide whether they had fulfilled their commitments. Their proposed section 36 would constitutionally entrench good intentions, not justiciable claims. Its legal status and practical application would continue to be negligible.

The Beaudoin-Dobbie report proposed to twin the social covenant with a set of commitments to an economic union. It would remove the existing commitments to equality and equalization from section 36 in doing this. One has to question the symbolic significance of new commitments to strengthen the economic union and promote full employment, reasonable standards of living and the free movement of persons, goods, services and capital when set alongside these deletions. It is not clear that the proposed section 36 is much of an improvement on the current one. The commitments to principles and goals read much like an election platform that any party or government could offer: much in the way of promise and little in the way of guaranteed delivery. Months of advocacy and debates over the social charter failed to produce meaningful entrenchment of economic-social rights. Since neither the Beaudoin-Dobbie Committee nor the Ontario government recognized that economic-social rights should be incorporated into the Charter of Rights as fundamental, enforceable rights, we can expect the fight over rights to continue.

Part IV: Constitutional Democracy

Chapter 14

Reforming National Political Institutions

Miriam Smith

Senate reform is seen as a way of giving the less populous regions greater weight in the central government. The so-called Triple-E Senate would be elected and effective in changing laws, and would give equal representation to all provinces. While equality of the provinces is unlikely to be accepted by either Ontario or Québec, the 1991 proposals did set out an elected Senate as a goal. In this chapter, Miriam Smith examines how a reformed Senate would affect the basic features of Canadian democracy, notably responsible government, and sets out criteria for evaluating institutional reform.

Canadians are increasingly alienated from their elected leaders and frustrated with their political institutions. This alienation manifests itself in high levels of voter volatility at the polls as well as in the rise of new political parties such as the Bloc Québécois and the Reform Party. Ironically, it is a right-wing party — the Reform Party — that has capitalized on the disaffection felt towards traditional political institutions. The Reform Party has revived the traditional demands of older Western protest parties (such as the Progressives) for a more democratic (and American) system of government, including a loosening or even abandonment of party discipline in the House of Commons and a Triple-E Senate. At the same time, disaffection with constitution making by back-room deal reached a historic high with the demise of the Meech Lake Accord.

Perhaps unsurprisingly, the Tories have chosen to respond to the democratic crisis in Canadian politics by moving in the direction of Reform Party proposals. The Tories have not adopted Reform's position wholesale, probably because many of Reform's proposals conflict with the basic tenets of parliamentary government. There is a limit on how far the Tories can accommodate Reform without jeopardizing institutional stability. But, in its 1991 constitutional proposals, the government has indicated its willingness to undertake reforms of Parliament including holding more free votes (and lessening party discipline) in the House, giving more power to parliamentary committees, and introducing an elected Senate with strong powers, although the precise balance of regional representation in the reformed upper chamber is left unspecified.

Nonetheless, the Tory proposals ignore a number of other ways that Canadian political institutions could be made more democratic. Unlike the Reform Party's agenda, many of these would not clash with our current parliamentary institutions. Stronger election financing laws, government funding of women, aboriginal and minority candidates, and proportional representation are all ways to make the political system more democratic, without creating institutional stalemate and instability. A democratic agenda for institutional reform should be based on a clear understanding of the basic rules of the game in a parliamentary system of government.

The Consequences of Responsible Government

The parliamentary system itself imposes strict limits on the extent to which the system can be democratized along the lines of traditional Western demands for more populist government.[1] Some of these demands would require not the reform of Canada's political institutions, but their wholesale dismantling. It is important to recognize that it is impossible simply to graft certain features of the U.S. system onto our political institutions without creating an unworkable and unstable governmental machinery.

The parliamentary system works in large part using a system of unwritten constitutional conventions that have not been codified in any of our Constitution Acts.[2] The most important of these is the doctrine of responsible government — that the prime minister and the cabinet must command the support of the House of Commons. If the government fails to command such support, it falls.

From this simple convention of the constitution, a number of consequences follow. First, there is a critical link between the legislature and the executive. Indeed, it is precisely this link that makes Canada a democracy. Without majority support in the House, the government is illegitimate. In contrast, in the U.S. system, there is no link between the executive and legislature; on the contrary, the U.S. system was devised with a separation of powers between the executive, legislative and judicial branches. Unlike the parliamentary system, the executive (the president) derives democratic legitimacy from direct election, independent of legislative elections. A defeat for the president's party in Congress does not require the resignation of the president.

A second consequence of this constitutional convention is that it gives political parties a very important role to play in maintaining the government. It is the parties that organize support for the prime minister and cabinet as well as opposition. Without at least some degree of party discipline, the government would be in constant danger of falling and, consequently, we would have frequent changes of government, frequent elections and a very unstable executive.

While party discipline is necessary to ensure the stability of the executive, it gives the prime minister and cabinet a great deal of authority over the legislative agenda. Indeed, the prime minister and cabinet have almost unbridled authority to legislate between elections.[3] As the government enjoys majority support in the House through the system of party discipline, the government has no incentive to compromise with its opposition. While this has the advantage of allowing the government to pursue a coherent agenda over its term in office, it also allows the government to pursue clearly unpopular policies for which it has no clear electoral mandate (as the Tories attempted to do with free trade). The difficulty is in finding a method of freeing MPs to vote against their own party that does not jeopardize the life of the government itself.[4]

The lack of party discipline and the independence of members of Congress are precisely the features that have long made the U.S. system attractive to Western populists. Indeed, members of Congress have much greater latitude to represent their constituents than do members of the House of Commons. From issue to issue, cross-party coalitions are constructed in the powerful congressional committees. Members of Congress are not required to vote with their party. Since, however (unlike the United States) the unravelling of the government's majority in the Canadian House of Commons would entail the resignation of the executive, the independence of the legislative representative in the U.S. system cannot be replicated to the same extent in our parliamentary system.

Furthermore, in the U.S. system, the independence of the member of Congress opens up the legislative system to strong pressures from interest and lobby groups. In the absence of strong election financing regulation, the U.S. Congress is susceptible to the influence of the groups with the most money, rather than to the democratic representation of the views and interests of members' constituents.

A third consequence of responsible government is that the prime minister and cabinet are responsible to only the House of Commons, where members are elected democratically based on territorial representation by population, and not to the Senate, whose members are appointed. If the Senate were reformed and made into a representative, elective chamber, then its powers with respect to confidence motions would have to be curtailed. The lower House must retain the decisive role in the making and unmaking of governments, if governmental paralysis is to be avoided.

The experience of Australia suggests that even with an elected, equal and effective Senate, the lower house still dominates the upper house and reduces its capacity to act as a regional representative. Australia employs the double dissolution as a means of resolving disputes and deadlocks between the two chambers. With the double dissolution, the governor-general, on the advice of the prime minister, dissolves both the Senate and the House. If the dispute is not resolved by the ensuing election, the deadlock is broken by a joint sitting of both chambers in which the disputed bills may be passed by a simple majority.

In practice, however, the political parties dominate the Australian Senate. Because there are fewer senators than members of the lower house, the party caucuses (for members of both chambers) are dominated by the members of the lower house, rather than by senators. In the event of deadlock, the power of dissolution is in the hands of the prime minister. Likewise, in a joint sitting of the two chambers, the members of the lower house outnumber senators by two to one. The Australian model resolves conflicts between the two houses, but at the expense of the Senate as both an effective chamber and as a chamber of regional representation.[5] This in turn suggests the difficulty of reconciling an effective Senate with responsible government. The onus is on supporters of a Triple-E Senate to show how paralysis and deadlock between the two "effective" chambers can be resolved.

Reforming the House: Towards an American System?

The Tories' reforms to the House of Commons would allow MPs greater autonomy in voting against their own party. The government would specify which of its measures are to be considered confidence votes by the House. On confidence votes, party discipline would still prevail. On other matters, however, MPs would have free votes; that is, they would not be bound by party discipline. This would allow MPs to better represent their regions and constituents. In addition, the government proposed that parliamentary committees be given more power to amend bills and that more time be allocated for private members' bills.

At this point, it is difficult to predict what the results of such reforms would be.[6] It largely depends on how far the government is willing to move towards a system of free votes in the House. The Tories suggested that confidence votes should be restricted to financial measures and other bills that are "central to the government's program."[7] Ultimately, the governing party would decide which votes are to be considered confidence votes; thus, the executive would still have a good deal of control over the legislative agenda and executive stability would be assured.

Nonetheless, it is worth speculating about the effects of loosening party discipline. First, it would be harder for all of the parties, including the opposition, to maintain unity. The parties may increasingly lose their partisan identities, as MPs deviate from the party line on some issues. This would make electoral politics in Canada more local, as voters no longer identify the parties with a legislative program. While this may bring government closer to the people, it may also muddy the choice between the parties.

Second, the system would be more open to public and interest-group pressure. While increased openness is to be welcomed, enforceable election spending limits must be in place to prevent powerful and monied groups from exerting undue influence over individual MPs.

Third, on issues that are subject to the free vote, the government would be forced to hammer out compromises with the opposition parties in order to get its legislation through the House. It is to be expected that such compromises would be devised in the reformed parliamentary committees, which would play a much more important role in the legislative process, particularly for amending bills. In this context, the parliamentary committees must be given substantial resources to hear from the public. Without strengthened public access to the committees, such compromises would become another series of backroom deals between politicians.

Nonetheless, the possibility of compromises between the governing party and the opposition on some legislation will make the House more responsive to public opinion. In sum, such a system might provide a balance between the need for a stable executive and the desire of Canadians to have more control over the majority party between elections.

Democratizing the Senate

The government has attempted to meet the demands for better representation of less populous regions with its proposal for an elected Senate, with elections to be held at the same time as elections to the House of Commons.

The government has not yet taken a position on the kind of electoral system that would be used for Senate elections. If the current first-past-the-post electoral system is used, it is likely that Senate elections will merely reproduce the balance of parties in the House of Commons, without significantly increasing the representation of minorities. As the main aim of the reformed Senate should be to provide representation to regions and to groups in Canadian society that are unrepresented or under-represented in the federal government, a system of proportional representation should be devised for Senate elections.

Such a system would ensure that significant minorities — NDP voters in Québec, Liberal voters in the West — receive Senate seats in proportion to their share of the popular vote. There would be less tendency for one party to dominate the Senate (as happens in the House), the parties would be much more balanced, different interests within each party would be represented, and small parties could gain a toehold in Parliament (it is easier for small parties to elect members under a proportional representation system).[8]

Along with a system of proportional representation, the government should establish financial incentives in our election financing laws to encourage women, ethnic minorities and aboriginal people to run for public office. All of these groups are seriously under-represented in both the Commons and the Senate under the current system. This could be combined with an overhaul of Canada's election-financing laws to curb the impact of corporate donations to the Liberal and Conservative parties and to ensure that interest-group spending in election campaigns — such as the pro-free trade campaign mounted by business groups during the 1988 election — is regulated.[9] If a system of proportional representation were used for Senate elections along with increased representation from under-represented groups, the reformed Senate would do more than simply reproduce the election results in the House; it would represent and express the views of significant minorities of Canadians who are currently neglected by the first-past-the-post system.

The government has left the very important question of the distribution of Senate seats among the provinces and territories to the committee process. It has stated that a redistribution of Senate seats should provide a more equitable representation for the less populous regions. An equal number of seats for each province would assuage the concerns of Westerners, but such a redistribution would mean that Ontario and Québec would lose influence in a reformed Senate.

The Tory proposal can be viewed as a compromise between the concerns expressed by Westerners over their lack of representation in federal political institutions and the concern of Québec not to be outvoted by the other nine provinces in a system of equal representation of provinces. The government's proposal that legislation affecting language or culture would require a double majority (both linguistic groups) is aimed at protecting Québec and the francophone minority outside Québec. A compromise of this type is probably the only way to secure the requisite provincial assent to Senate reform and to balance the claims of the regions.

Another important aspect of the Tory proposal is that the powers of the Senate would be much more clearly specified than they are at present. Currently, the Senate has an absolute veto over legislation, although it has rarely exercised it. The 1991 proposals would give the elected Senate a six-month suspensive veto over all government legislation except financial bills. This means that the House of Commons could override the Senate veto after six months.

These restrictions on the Senate's powers provide a way to avoid conflicts between the two legislative chambers and to ensure the stability of the executive between elections. In this manner, the federal proposals circumvent the need for the double dissolution and other measures for resolving deadlocks that are found in the Australian model but at the risk of undermining the complete "effectiveness" of the new Senate.

On the other hand, the six-month suspensive veto, like the loosening of party discipline in the House, would institutionalize an inducement for the governing party to compromise with its opposition in order to get legislation through the Senate. As the Senate would have much more democratic legitimacy as an elected and representative chamber, Senate opposition to government measures would galvanize public opinion and increase the visibility and openness of government. In particular, for measures that are designated as confidence measures in the House (and these are likely to be the most important measures), the Senate's suspensive veto would provide a useful check on the power of the executive. While the suspensive veto could be overridden by the government in the Commons after six months, there would be many occasions when the government might be willing to compromise with its opponents in order to expedite the passage of its legislation.

The Council of the Federation: More Power for Governments

With the proposed reforms to the House and Senate, the government has taken some steps towards democratizing government at the national level. However, constitutionalizing federal-provincial relations in the proposed Council of the Federation would increase the power of provincial governments in the federal system. Unlike Senate reform, which provides democratic representation of regional concerns in the national government, the Council of the Federation would increase the power of governments rather than the power of people.

The Council would play a very significant role in developing economic and social policy in Canada. In the 1991 Mulroney-Clark proposals, it is suggested that the Council would have to approve the federal government's exercise of its new economic powers, as well as the establishment of future shared-cost (social) programmes and fiscal harmonization between different levels of government. The government proposed that the federal exercise of such powers should be subject to the approval of seven provinces with 50 percent of the population (the "seven and 50" rule), as are some types of constitutional amendment (including the government's constitutional proposals). The government thus proposed to create a new "amending formula," complete with opting-out provisions for provinces, which could be renewed after three years.

While the government claimed that the establishment of the Council of the Federation would increase the visibility of intergovernmental negotiation, the establishment and constitutional entrenchment of such a Council would in no way increase the visibility of the process. The government would be constitutionalizing a behind-closed-doors process of intergovernmental negotiation at the same time as it established new economic goals — fiscal harmonization and the free flow of people, goods, services and capital. The entrenchment of such an institution in the constitution would tie the hands of future governments. The ability of Canadians to control government and to make choices about alternative futures through the electoral system would be diminished.

Democratizing the System

The Tory proposals were an attempt to deal with both regional demands for greater representation at the centre as well as with the general disenchantment towards political institutions among voters. While the constitutional proposals took steps in the direction of greater democracy, in particular for the Senate and the House of Commons, the entrenchment of intergovernmental negotiation in the Council of the Federation would be a step in the other direction.

There is much more to be done. Until now, the Reform Party has captured the high ground on the issue of reforming and democratizing our political institutions. Surely it is time for a genuine democracy agenda. Such an agenda should include a Senate elected by proportional representation; government funding of women, aboriginal and minority candidates; and, most important, strong limits on election spending that would take the electoral process back from the business interest groups that helped secure the Tory victory in 1988. An electoral system that can be subverted by wealth is profoundly undemocratic. Finally, a democratic agenda must focus on social rights as a non-negotiable component of democratic citizenship, along the lines suggested by the Ontario government's Social Charter proposals. The left must not allow the Reform Party to define the agenda of democratization.

Chapter 15

The West Wants In

Philip Resnick

Western Canada is often seen as speaking with one voice when it calls for a greater say in national affairs. A notable example of this is its strong support for Senate reform. In fact, there are important differences between the social democrats who were governing British Columbia and Saskatchewan during the final stages of debate on the Mulroney-Clark proposals, and the conservatives who held sway in Alberta and Manitoba. Therefore, although it is clear that Western views of the constitutional process have had a significant impact on the federal proposals, the ideological gap between left and right in the West could translate into divisions on important questions. In this chapter, Philip Resnick examines Western attitudes to specific aspects of the 1991 proposals and suggests that there may be some surprises to come out of the concern for democracy being expressed by left and right alike.

One of the great myths of the constitutional debate of 1991–92 is that there is a single West. To listen to some of the supporters of the Reform Party of Canada (for example, columnists for Reform-leaning magazines like *Alberta Report* and *B.C. Report*) or spokespersons for the Calgary-based Canada West Foundation, one would assume an undiluted Western voice from Manitoba's border with Ontario to the Queen Charlotte Islands. This West would seem to demand more power in national affairs, through a Triple-E Senate and through the devolution of many existing federal powers to the provinces; would oppose any recognition of Québec's distinct character; would be wary of any open-ended commitment to aboriginal rights; and would be strongly predisposed to the defence of private property and to rolling back the sphere of government activity.

Yet there is another West, whose origins go back to agrarian and labour protest movements of the early twentieth century, and which finds expression in the policies of the NDP governments in British Columbia and Saskatchewan. This West is less committed to whittling away federal powers the better to strengthen the provinces; is far more favourable to the values of community and sharing than to a purely market-driven notion of society; was strongly opposed to the free trade agreement and to the accompanying risks of Canada's wholesale Americanization; is relatively open to the notion of aboriginal rights; and recognizes the importance of preserving some ongoing Canada-Québec political arrangement into the future.

There are, nonetheless, a number of issues on which Westerners from right to left, from the Reform Party to the NDP, probably do agree. There is a commitment to a more democratic process of constitution making, of the constituent assembly and referendum variety. There is concern that, as a region, the West get its fair share of input into national decision making and that the federal government and Parliament better reflect the demographic weight of the close to 8 million Western Canadians. To this extent, the Reform Party's "The West Wants

In" slogan has an appeal far beyond the ranks of its right-of-centre supporters. And Westerners believe in a Canada that is more than the sum of its parts, and oppose special status for any province or region within our existing federal structures.

This brings me to the Mulroney-Clark constitutional proposals tabled in September 1991, in *Shaping Canada's Future Together*. How have Westerners responded to the federal package?

Let me begin with process. Nowhere did the closed door, top-down process of constitution making associated with Meech offend as much as in Western Canada. Grass roots movements committed to direct democracy in this part of the country go back to the Progressives and United Farmers of Alberta. The notion that a document as important as a constitution — that is, a social contract by which governments, no less than citizens, are bound — could somehow be rewritten without public consultation rubs against the grain. This means that there will be profound suspicion of any document which is not the result of a transparently democratic process. By this standard, the Conservative proposals, hatched behind closed doors over the summer of 1991, fail almost as badly as Meech. Nor will a joint parliamentary committee with a built-in Conservative majority (the Beaudoin-Dobbie Committee, which travelled the country business class) mollify the many Westerners who told the Spicer Commission, the Beaudoin-Edwards Joint Parliamentary Committee and anyone else who cared to listen that they wanted direct input into the process. *Plus ça change* ...

The proposals do make a significant move towards Senate reform and towards freer votes in the House of Commons, both of which will be welcome. Yet the specifics of Senate reform may prove more controversial than the principle of direct election itself. Are we talking about equal representation for all provinces — with Prince Edward Island having the same number of senators as Ontario or British Columbia? This has been the bottom-line credo of many in Alberta, and of the Reform Party in particular. But it may well be that an effective Senate must be one that better represents the demographic weight of the different regions and provinces, even while ensuring that the peripheries (the West, Atlantic Canada, the North) outweigh Québec and Ontario. This suggests a sliding scale for Senate membership, with greater blocs from a first tier of provinces like Ontario and Québec, somewhat smaller contingents from second-tier ones like British Columbia and Alberta, and still less for the smaller provinces. Equally contentious may be the issues of whether Senate elections are to be by proportional representation or from constituencies, and whether they are to be held at the same time as elections to the House of Commons or as provincial elections. And the hoary question as to whether an elected Senate ought to have a suspensive veto over all legislation, including financial, and an absolute veto in constitutional matters, will divide opinion.

On aboriginal self-government, views in the West — with the largest relative concentration of aboriginal people south of 60 — will vary. Overall, there is greater receptiveness to aboriginal demands than ever before, in part, interestingly enough, because of Elijah Harper's courageous role in blocking Meech. Once one turns to specifics, however, and issues like land claims, treaty rights and self-government come up for negotiation, the apparent unanimity will dissolve. In general, New Democrats and Liberals in the West are more prepared to make substantial concessions in these areas than are those on the right of the political spectrum.

As regards the distinct society clause, the heart of our recent constitutional *malheurs,* there is a deep scepticism running across the region. Bourassa's invocation of the "notwithstanding clause" on the sign law has left bitter wounds. It was as though Québec were no longer bound by the Official Languages Act where its anglophone minority was concerned, even though the West, reluctantly at first, had bought into official bilingualism. It also seemed to Westerners as though the Charter of Rights would mean one thing in Canada outside Québec and something different within Québec.

This is why I have grave doubts whether the 1991 Conservative constitutional proposals, despite the more carefully circumscribed character of the "distinct society" this time around, will pass muster in the West. For many, the distinct society clause still smacks of special status, particularly when one adds to this the powers over immigration and culture that Québec stands to acquire through sections 19 and 20. It is also worth underlining the fact that in British Columbia at the moment — and will other Western provinces be far behind? — there is a statutory requirement that any constitutional changes, before they are approved by the legislature, be first submitted for popular approval in a referendum. Any bets on the likely outcome?

Still, there may be more of an opening to Québec in Western Canadian public opinion than the tarnished language of "distinct society" can ever evoke. What Westerners will not stand for are special privileges for one province as against the others. But there is fairly broad recognition that in language, culture and much besides, Québec is truly different. It just may be that Westerners may prove open to a new constitutional arrangement with Québec, with the proviso that in all areas in which Québec acquires enhanced jurisdiction the *quid pro quo* would be no further say for Québec where the rest of Canada is concerned. Québec cannot have it both ways. If it wants recognition of its national distinctiveness, and some or all of the powers that the Allaire Report of the Québec Liberal Party talked about, the price will be a drastically reduced Québec role in Ottawa. Call this asymmetrical federalism, if you wish, or call it a still-to-be-fleshed-out confederal-type arrangement. Either way there may be more support for radical alternatives like these in Western Canada than for a distinct society clause with its slippery-slope ambiguity.

On the economic union, Western Canadian premiers, whether Conservative or NDP, are likely to be opposed; so, quite frankly, is much of public opinion. While there is a case for reducing provincial barriers to the circulation of people and goods, the suspicion is that the proposal represents a power-grab by Ottawa. There will also be questions as to why it is only the economic union that the Conservative government seems to want to strengthen, as opposed to the cultural, social and symbolic dimensions of Canadian nationhood.

The deepest cleavages within Western public opinion crystallize around three issues: the property clause in section 1; the increased role of the provinces in matters like Supreme Court nominations (section 12), housing (section 27), the environment (section 26), residual powers (section 22) and the like; and the proposed Council of the Federation (section 28), a new third level of political decision making.

Other contributors to this volume have addressed some of these issues at greater length. With respect to property, suffice it to say that Westerners of a left or liberal persuasion (a substantial part of the population of the four provinces) will oppose any entrenchment of property rights in the Charter. This is not because they harbour wicked intentions; our common law tradition, in any case, would make it impossible to proceed down some confiscatory route. The real motive for their opposition is that a property clause could become a tremendous obstacle to the type of land claim negotiations, environmental regulations or gender equality legislation that, more and more, must be the order of the day. It would also make the more communitarian features of Canadian public life harder to foster and maintain.

Conversely, and one must frankly recognize this, any calls for a social charter from NDP governments would spark equally strong resistance from those on the right — Reform and Conservative, and even many Liberals — who would not want to recognize, let alone constitutionalize, so-called social rights. There might eventually be some kind of a trade-off between property and social rights. On this issue, controversy will rage and polarize opinion.

The question of the division of powers is the sleeper in the package, little likely, at first blush, to stir deep passions. Let us not forget, however, that a good deal of the anti-Meech sentiment in English Canada was provoked by a sense that the powers of the federal government were going to be significantly eroded. There are many in Western Canada, regardless of ethnic origin or province of residence, whose first and foremost loyalty is to Canada. They are not particularly interested in seeing provincial premiers, whose limitations, alas, they know all too well, acquire undue influence over national affairs. *Shaping Canada's Future Together* will do just that where Supreme Court appointments are concerned. This, despite the fact that we would now get an elected Senate, better reflecting the regional principle at the centre. Why has the reformed Senate not been given the power of vetting Supreme Court appointees in the constitutional proposals?

What are the implications, moreover, for agencies like the CMHC and for national housing standards, of giving the provinces complete control over housing? Or of "streamlining," i.e., provincializing, wildlife conservation and protection, or soil and water conservation? After the Rafferty-Alameda Dam fiasco, do Westerners concerned about the environment trust provincial politicians with such powers? And the residual power? Where is the hue and cry across the West to have this transferred to the provinces?

In truth, the Conservative government is following the same decentralizing "community of communities" agenda that underlay Meech. And there are members of the Canada West Foundation, of the B.C. Social Credit Party, and movers and shakers in the corporate power structure of Calgary or Vancouver like Peter Lougheed or Gordon Gibson, Jr., who would like to see a wholesale devolution of powers take place.

But is theirs really the "voice of the people"? How does one explain majority opposition to any shift in federal powers to the provinces across English-speaking Canada, including the West (*Globe*/CBC poll, April 22, 1991)? How does one explain the sentiments in favour of national standards in education that the Spicer Commission heard in its Western hearings? Or the significant number of intervenors before the Alberta Legislative Committee on the Constitution defending the role of the federal government? There is far greater support for a strong, central government across Western Canada than meets the eye, something the current sense of national crisis will, if anything, reinforce.

It is for precisely this reason that I doubt a majority in the West will easily buy the Council of the Federation proposal in the Conservative package. This idea was the brainchild of Mel Smith, hired gun in constitutional matters for successive B.C. Social Credit governments. It would institutionalize the equivalent of federal-provincial conferences as a permanent feature of political decision making in this country, where the economic union, future federal-provincial cost sharing programmes and similar matters were concerned. One of the main criticisms of Meech, which the Conservatives have chosen to ignore, was that it would have institutionalized annual federal-provincial constitutional conferences into the indefinite future. Why would the public take lightly to this new proposal? The only clear beneficiaries would be operators like Mel Smith who make a living out of federal-provincial conflict, and unabashed proponents of greater provincial power in the mould of Bill Vander Zalm or Grant Devine. The mood in the West, at the moment, fortunately is running against provincial power barons.

Let me conclude with a prediction. The 1991 federal proposals are so weighted down with baggage from the discredited past like the distinct society clause from Meech Lake, or complex and controversial proposals like the property clause, Senate reform, the economic union and the Council of the Federation, that they are unlikely to secure easy passage. If they fail — and the chances are at least 50–50 of this happening, if not higher — what lies ahead? The doom and gloom that the Tories were predicting when Meech failed? The complete separation of Québec from Canada, following a referendum, an election, or both?

There is another possible scenario. This is the constituent assembly route which Mulroney, Clark and their allies in both government and the media have done everything to block. Yet this option has garnered the support of about 60 percent of English-speaking Canadians in public opinion surveys ever since the demise of Meech Lake. There are now three provincial governments in Western Canada — those of Manitoba, Saskatchewan and British Columbia — who would support a constituent assembly proposal if the Mulroney-Clark proposals fail, and a fourth, Alberta's, likely to fall into line given overwhelming public support for the idea in that province. The West — here, at least, speaking with one voice across the ideological divide — will be a very powerful force in pushing Canada, or at least English-speaking Canada, in the direction of democratic constitution making. And it may be precisely through some future constituent assembly — largely elected, if you please — that the West will do its bit in helping to bring English-speaking Canada together, and to lay the foundation for a new political relationship between Canada and Québec and between non-native and aboriginal peoples in this country. Then Westerners, like all Canadians, will really be in.

Chapter 16

Beyond Brokerage Politics: Towards the Democracy Round

Jane Jenson

Democracy is an important political value, all agree, yet when the democratic test is applied to recent constitutional history, the results are disappointing. In this chapter, Jane Jenson assesses the government's 1991 proposals and finds the entrenchment of a neo-conservative agenda that will mean future governments, both provincial and federal, will be limited in the kinds of decisions they can make. Governments that are stalemated leave more space for corporations. Jenson calls for an approach that would reduce the influence on government of the powerful and privileged, in favour of alternative political visions. What should be clear after the Meech Lake debate is that Canadians want their voices heard throughout the constitutional reform process and beyond.

A constitution is not something that affects only the realm of "high politics." After the long years of Canada's constitutional odyssey we are finally recognizing this fact. Making decisions about our constitutional future is *not* an activity that we have to get over before we can get on with the real issues of everyday life: jobs, taxes, education, trade or whatever. At this point in the history of this country *constitution making is everyday politics*. By choosing among constitutional options today we are already making choices about what will be feasible tomorrow and possible into the longer future.

Constitutions are declarations about desirable presents and futures. Even if written in a language that is complicated and legalistic, constitutions are statements of political ideals and concrete arrangements for translating them into practice. They set out a vision of who we are and who we might be. In other words, constitutions are a major way in which societies represent themselves to themselves.

Constitutions provide, therefore, a representation of democratic citizenship. Definitions of citizenship matter because they organize popular understandings of the relationship between the individual and the state. They describe the rights and duties of citizens as well as designating the responsibility of the state for protecting citizens and their rights. Most importantly, such definitions permit and encourage certain ways of making claims upon the government and of empowering groups and categories of citizens.

Contestation over citizenship rights is most likely to occur precisely at those moments when the relationship between the citizen and the state is undergoing substantial alteration, just as it is now in this time of constitution making. It is at such moments that groups can make new and novel claims for a more democratic citizenship which recognizes the diversity of citizens and their needs.

Because constitution making involves such contestation about the meaning of citizenship and democracy and because we already know that there are widely different competing visions of the things which are most valuable about this country and its history, it is important that everyone — but especially those who do not share the Conservative government's perspective — intervene in the constitutional discussion. Moments such as these provide an opportunity to introduce alternative visions and to allow new voices to make their claims heard.

This constitutional round will decide whether constitutional law will severely limit the future space for enacting decisions made within the institutions of democratic politics, at both provincial and federal levels. If the Tories' proposals are adopted, this generation as well as those coming after will be compelled to live according to a neo-conservative doctrine that celebrates market forces and abdicates any possibility of political action to control, shape and mediate the impact of the market.

An alternative does exist, however. It is one which would maintain and create democratic political processes by enhancing the possibility of really debating constitutional choices and accommodating diverse viewpoints, both during this round of constitutional politics and into the future. If this alternative were pursued, the current round of negotiations could become the *democracy round.*

Entrenching Neo-Conservatism

The proposals put forward by the Tory government in 1991 were designed to write into the constitution the government's own policy preferences. By elevating neo-conservative principles to constitutional dogma, they endeavoured to ensure continued low levels of social spending, massive unemployment and solicitude for the demands of business at the expense of ordinary Canadians. By trying to write neo-conservatism into the constitution, the Mulroney Tories want to guarantee that they will tie the hands of *all* future governments, both federal and provincial. It will become exceedingly difficult for democratically elected and citizen-directed governments to design an economic future which involves paying more attention to unemployment than to inflation, protecting provincial development from external economic forces, designing their own budgets and developing coherent political projects that reject a neo-conservative vision.

How do the proposals do this? Most obvious is the entrenchment of property rights. While this celebration of property might seem initially appealing, it is important to recognize that more is at stake than simply protection of one's house or farm. Guaranteeing property rights could allow individuals and corporations to allege that they have the right to pollute or to deforest their property even when aboriginal peoples have historic claims to the same property. More importantly, entrenching property rights with no corresponding acknowledgement of social rights means recognizing the individual and ignoring the collectivity, recognizing private ownership and ignoring the reality of interconnections in an ecologically sensitive and socially complex world.

It is not only the property rights clause which would entrench neo-conservatism, however. There is also the provision that would make the Bank of Canada guarantee "price stability" (that is, control inflation) but ignore measures for job creation or other equally important economic goals. In this way the Bank would be able to further hinder efforts by a democratically elected government to direct monetary policy towards progressive ends.

The most elaborate expression of this neo-conservative agenda is found in the proposals for the so-called stronger economic union. The first thing to note about these proposals is that they will *not* make any government stronger. They are not mechanisms for centralizing power, even though they are a means of disempowering the provinces.

The Tories' document proposed to make "interprovincial barriers to trade" unconstitutional. In effect, this means instituting free trade among the provinces. With such a constitutional change, it would become impossible to use some of the policy mechanisms which provincial governments have deployed in order to undertake development strategies. From that time on, policies designed to give provincial residents access to jobs, to encourage industrial or other forms of development, to cushion and manage economic restructuring, all could be challenged before the courts as "restraints on trade" or "unfair subsidies." They could be struck down as unconstitutional.

Of course, as we move into the twenty-first century, Canada must adapt to the pressures of globalization and increased international competition. In that context it is difficult to argue that Canada should not follow the trend towards more open markets and freer trade. However, the Tories' strategy is simply to let the market decide and to allow restructuring that conforms purely to the preferences of business, whether national or transnational. This is not the only way to adjust to the new international economic and political situation. The government's proposal failed to recognize that such adaptation might be done in ways which do not completely eliminate the possibility of exercising control over economic restructuring. It is possible to preserve space for democratically selected strategies that respond to the new circumstances of global competition. Yet all that the Tories proposed was simply to allow the market to rule. As the experience of the European Community clearly demonstrates, even if a single market is created, it remains feasible — and for the Europeans, important — to make sure that at least one level of government retains the ability to act. The European example, at least, shows that a system of internal free trade which still permits political decisions about development strategies is imaginable and practical.

Maintenance of such space for politics in this country might involve doing at least two things. First, positive actions by provincial governments to promote development would have to be explicitly excluded from the constitutional ban on restraints on trade. This means that clear definitions of "restraint" and "fair subsidy" would have to be developed — in advance of any new constitutional agreement. As we know, these crucial matters were left undefined in the Canada-U.S. free trade agreement in 1988, and that absence continues to threaten our future. Such clear definitions would then give provincial governments elected on platforms promising specific economic development strategies the power to implement them without having to fight off constitutional challenges.

Second, and even more importantly, if the provinces are to lose some of their economic powers in the name of the so-called economic union, these powers must be *relocated.* They cannot simply be eliminated. If they are, no government — provincial or federal — will be able to act.

The Tories' proposal was one which would make it virtually impossible for any government to co-ordinate national economic policy. By making the proposed Council of the Federation responsible for economic oversight and by invoking the "seven and 50" rule for decision making, the plan was a recipe for stalemate.

The Conservatives do not mind that stalemate is the most likely outcome, because they do not believe that governments should act in positive ways to extend equity, protect the weak, create economic well-being and help to shape our futures. They do not mind tying the hands of future democratically elected federal and provincial governments. The Tories believe in buccaneer capitalism.

But anyone who does not share this economic ideology has reason to be worried by this plan for making national economic policy via the amending formula. Redesigning the constitution according to these rules for "economic union" is most likely to mean the continuation of these past years of market-driven politics. Any federal government that wished to do otherwise would have to generate the same level of consensus for a simple change in economic policy as has been required since 1982 to make an amendment to the Constitution Act.

This entrenchment of the neo-conservative agenda in the constitution represents a fundamental shift in visions of citizenship. In Canada's past, such visions have always included support for the idea of the collectivity; they have never exclusively celebrated the rights of individuals and economic liberalism. Such ideals have found expression in a greater trust in democratically driven state action to shape market relations in the name of social solidarity as well as in guarantees of collective rights. It is this vision of a more collective citizenship that the Tories' proposals challenged. The constitutional proposals subordinated democratic expressions of collective solidarity to the forces of market liberalism.

Making This Round the Democracy Round

The politicians have learned their lesson, after the uproar over the undemocratic procedures by which the Meech Lake Accord was designed and the widespread evidence of fundamental hostility against politicians. This time they have offered "consultations." This new attitude is a major improvement. The politicians have been forced to listen to alternative visions of solidarity, democracy and citizenship.

Given this process, it should be possible to make the discussion one which is more democratic in its procedures and which might embed real democratic institutions in the constitution.

On both these counts, however, the Tories' proposals fell short of complete success. As other chapters clearly indicate, the suggested reforms did extend democracy, when they accepted Senate reform. Yet at the same time they proposed setting up a new and important institution which is not elected and which simply formalizes the élitism of executive federalism. If the Council of the Federation were to be created, it would elevate to constitutional status the existing practices in which federal-provincial agreements made by eleven first ministers — and even by non-elected bureaucrats — tie the hands of elected federal and provincial legislators. Parliament or the provincial legislatures can only rubber-stamp — or reject — such agreements. The Meech Lake events demonstrated how awkward and even painful were the consequences of weakening the power of parliamentary institutions and of reducing the space for debate to the right to say "no."

Even more telling of the lack of a real commitment to democracy is the fashion in which the government proceeded in designing these proposals. It treated the crucial decisions of constitution making as nothing more than another opportunity for brokering among interests.

The Tories proudly announced that their proposals were a delicate balance. What they resemble much more is an effort to buy off as many interests as possible by tossing a bone here, a bone there, in the hope that everyone will be satisfied with a little. The proposals lacked any coherent vision of a truly democratic future and had little that would provide a redefinition of citizenship for the twenty-first century.

This definition of politics as simply *brokering* reflects not only Mulroney's approach to politics-as-negotiation. It is also an expression of a much more deeply embedded assumption that principles do not really count. This definition has long dominated federal politics. In this view, politics is primarily symbolic politics. Rarely are alternative visions or projects for representing the whole country clearly presented. Moreover, in this view, politics is best conducted among "experts," and then in backrooms where horse-trading can take place far from public scrutiny.

The 1991 proposals and constitutional discussion provide ample evidence that this vision of politics continues to dominate constitution making. While the Tories may be trying to entrench their own neo-conservative economic agenda in the constitution, they are also willing to let it be known that "changes are possible," that the essential elements of the package are negotiable and might be redesigned.

Such *ad hoc* efforts at redesign are not evidence of a commitment to democracy, however. Nor will they produce a coherent replacement. Rather, they are simply attempts to grease the squeaky wheels. Those who can put pressure can force changes. Those citizens who are less important to the Tories — the poor, the unemployed and women, for example, who are less likely to vote for them — have much less power to force changes.

An alternative understanding of more democratic constitution making pushes the discussion out of the bureaucrats' offices and the backrooms and into the open, where real accommodations can be made only after the consequences for everyone have been fully assessed. Such an alternative view of politics, translated into constitution writing, challenges the assumption that politics is simply about brokering. It involves, instead, a discussion of first principles, one which assesses the implications of choices and rejects last minute "add-ons" which appease powerful interests at the cost of the weak. Such an approach reduces the influence of those who are now most powerful and who have the ear of the government. It would empower citizens more than any previous efforts have done.

Undertaking constitution making in this way would begin to move our traditional brokerage politics towards democratic participation and democratic debate. It would open up the process to voices which are seldom heard in the closed rooms of executive federalism and Cabinets. Constitution making would become a process of accommodating difference, of accepting the diversity which characterizes the country. It would provide a way for citizens to recognize one another in all their distinctiveness as well as to identify what they have in common.

If the procedure of consultation by parliamentary committee that was initiated in 1991 should fail, we cannot return to past practices of bureaucratic manoeuvring and closed-door negotiations among the first ministers. Rather, the time will clearly have arrived to consider more innovative procedures. Proposals for a constituent assembly bringing together citizens from all over the country have attracted much attention since the failure of the Meech Lake Accord. Many citizens now understand that this may be the last, best chance for them to take control of and design their own futures. They are claiming the right for Canadians to represent ourselves to ourselves by setting out a popular vision of what the constitution should say about our future. They are coming to recognize that the only worthwhile effort is one which attempts to craft a constitutional document which represents the accommodations which all of us are willing to make in order to share this space from sea to sea to sea.

Notes

Chapter Two

1. Frank R. Scott, "French Canada and Canadian Federation," in *Evolving Canadian Federalism,* ed. A. R. M. Loower, F. R. Scott et al. (Durham, N.C.: Duke University Press, 1958), 57.
2. Royal Commission on Bilingualism and Biculturalism, *Preliminary Report* (Ottawa: Queen's Printer, 1965), 127.
3. François Rocher, "Pour un réaménagement du régime constitutionnel: Québec d'abord!" in *Daniel Johnson: Rêve d'égalité et projet d'indépendance,* ed. R. Comeau, M. Lévesque and Y. Bélanger (Sillery: Presses de l'Université du Québec, 1991).
4. Alain-G. Gagnon and Mary Beth Montcalm, *Québec: Beyond the Quiet Revolution* (Scarborough, Ont.: Nelson Canada, 1990), 158.
5. José Voehrling, "L'échec de l'Accord du Lac Meech et l'avenir constitutionnel du Canada," in *Canada on the Threshold of the 21st Century,* ed. C. H. V. Remie and J. M. Lacroix (Amsterdam/Philadelphia: John Benjamins, 1991), 393-96.

Chapter Five

1. The Canadian constitution, together with judicial interpretation, guaranteed a customs union together with an "imperfect" common market for goods, capital and enterprise. See T. J. Courchene, "Analytical Perspectives on the Canadian Economic Union," *Federalism and the Canadian Economic Union,* ed. M. J. Trebilcock, J. R. S. Prichard, T. J. Courchene and J. Whalley (Toronto: University of Toronto Press for the Ontario Economic Council, 1983), 65. To this may be added federal-provincial and interprovincial agreements and the Canadian Charter of Rights and Freedoms, which reinforce aspects of the economic union. See T. J. Cour-

chene, *In Praise of Renewed Federalism* (Toronto: C. D. Howe Institute, 1991), 12–13.

2. These are identified in the federal document, *Canadian Federalism and Economic Union: Partnership for Prosperity* (Ottawa: Supply and Services, 1991), 19, 43–45.
3. According to Whalley, economists use the term *distortion* as a popular synonym for *barrier.* But most use *distortion* "to describe a policy that is discriminatory, in the sense that it treats participants in transactions differently." See John Whalley, "Induced Distortions of Interprovincial Activity," in T. J. Courchene et al., 162–63.
4. See M. J. Trebilcock, J. Whalley. C. Rogerson, and I. Ness, "Provincially Induced Barriers to Trade in Canada," in M. J. Trebilcock et al., 294–95, 302–4.
5. See the Alberta Insurance Act, R.S.A. 1980, c.I-5, s.94(3) and Trebilcock et al., 299.
6. As in the province of Saskatchewan. See Trebilcock et al., 261.
7. See the Alberta Resources Preservation Act, R.S.A. 1980, c.G-3.1, ss.8–9.
8. A "barrier to the economic union includes any initiative that alters the wage/rental rate or the leisure/labour choice or the tax price of public goods on a geographical basis." See T. J. Courchene, *In Praise of Renewed Federalism*, 14.
9. Although a 1979 federal study concluded that there is "little evidence to suggest that their impact is a *major barrier* to labour mobility." Discussed in Trebilcock, et al., 286.
10. See Trebilcock et al., 314.
11. Trebilcock et al., 285–86.
12. According to the federal government document on the economic union, impediments to mobility include unintentional policies such as "non-harmonized regulation of environmental standards." See *Canadian Federalism and Economic Union*, 17.

13. I am grateful to Professor Elaine Hughes for this example.
14. See "Powers Over the Economy: Securing the Canadian Economic Union in the Constitution," in *The Constitution Act 1982 & Amendments: A Documentary History*, ed. A. Bayefsky (Toronto: McGraw-Hill Ryerson, 1989), 607.
15. See *Canadian Federalism and the Economic Union*, 19.
16. See *Gold Seal Ltd.* v. *A.G. Alberta* (1921) 62 S.C.R. 424 and *R. v. Nat Bell Liquors Ltd.*, [1922] 2 A.C. 128. Broader interpretations can be found in *Murphy v. C.P.R.*, [1958] S.C.R. 626, *Reference re Agricultural Products Marketing Act*, [1978] 2 S.C.R. 1198 per Laskin CJ, and *Black v. Law Society of Alberta*, [1989] 1 S.C.R. 591.
17. Canadian Bar Association Committee on the Constitution, *Towards a New Canada* (Montreal: The Canadian Bar Foundation, 1978), 85ff.
18. The Task Force on Canadian Unity, *A Future Together* (Ottawa: Supply and Services, 1979), 67–70.
19. The Constitutional Committee of the Quebec Liberal Party, *A New Canadian Federation* (Montreal: Quebec Liberal Party, 1980), 105.
20. *Supra*, note 14. A useful history of this proposal is found in Annex B to 616–19.
21. See Royal Commission on the Economic Union and Development Prospects for Canada, *Report*, vol. 3 (Ottawa: Supply and Services, 1985), 136–40. Calls for an economic union were also made in the Report of the Group of 22, *Some Practical Suggestions for Canada* (Montreal: le Groupe Columbia, June 1991), 20; Canadian Manufacturers' Association, " 'Canada 1993': A Plan for the Creation of a Single Market in Canada" (April 1991); and Canada West Foundation, "Time for Action: Reducing Interprovincial Barriers to Trade" (May 1989).

22. Report of the Constitutional Committee of the Quebec Liberal Party, *A Quebec Free to Choose* (January 28, 1991), 36.
23. Richard Fidler, trans. and ed., *Canada, Adieu? Quebec Debates Its Future* (Vancouver and Halifax: Oolichan Books and Institute for Research on Public Policy, 1991), 84.
24. See *Canadian Federalism and Economic Union*, 21.
25. These, and other reasons, are discussed in K. Norrie, R. Simeon, and M. Krasnick, *Federalism and the Economic Union in Canada* (Toronto: University of Toronto Press, 1986), 249–51.
26. Some discussion can be found in J. A. Hayes, *Economic Mobility in Canada: A Comparative Study* (Ottawa: Supply and Services, 1982) and A. E. Safarian, *Canadian Federalism and Economic Integration* (Ottawa: Information Canada, 1974).
27. Peter Hanks, *Australian Constitutional Law: Materials and Commentary*, 4th ed. (Sydney: Butterworths, 1990), 689.
28. See *Uebergang v. Australian Wheat Board* (1980), 145 C.L.R. 226 at 300.
29. (Australian Government Publishing Service, 1987), 206.
30. A. E. Safarian, 20.
31. See *Towards a New Canada*, 88.
32. See *Cole v. Whitfield* (1988), 78 A.L.R. 42 at 48.
33. See T. Lee and M. J. Trebilcock, "Economic Mobility and Constitutional Reform" (1987) 37 U.T.L.J. 268 at 312.
34. See Ontario, *A Canadian Social Charter: Making Our Shared Values Stronger* (Toronto: Ministry of Intergovernmental Affairs, 1991), 8.
35. According to Peter Leslie, "the presence of the US on our doorstep requires adaptive behaviour by Canada; efforts to buck continental trends will be damaging and counter-productive." *The European Community: A Political Model for Canada?* (Ottawa: Supply and Services, 1991), 31.

36. Ibid., 33.
37. See *Citizen's Forum on Canada's Future, Report to the People and Government of Canada* (Ottawa: Supply and Services, 1991), 132, where the Spicer Commission found that Canadians look to their governments to play a role in redressing market imperfections and supplementing market initiatives.
38. The same problems do not arise when the federal government invokes its s.91(2) power over "trade and commerce." But there is no discussion in the federal proposals about how this power may be exercised in conjunction with the new s.91A power. Might the federal government be legally, if not morally, obliged to obtain the consent of a majority of provinces before it exercises the general trade and commerce power it previously could exercise unilaterally?
39. W. H. Furtan, "Agriculture in a Restructured Canada" (Western Centre for Economic Research: The Economics of Constitutional Change Series, Art. #3, June 1991), 7.
40. See Report of the Advisory Council on Adjustment, *Choosing to Win* (Ottawa: Supply and Services, 1989).
41. The Manitoba Constitutional Task Force recently recommended that political action be taken to remove interprovincial economic barriers. See *Report of the Manitoba Constitutional Task Force* (October 28, 1991), 52–54.
42. See Charles Macli, "Duelling in the Dark," *Report on Business Magazine* (April 1991):29.

Chapter Eight

1. *Canadian Federalism and Economic Union: Partnership for Prosperity* (Ottawa: Minister of Supply and Services, 1991) 11.
2. Ibid.
3. Ibid., 11
4. *The Financial Post* (September 29, 1991): A4.
5. *Canadian Federalism and Economic Union*, 11.

6. Canadian Manufacturers' Association, *"Canada 1993" A Plan for the Creation of a Single Economic Market in Canada* (April 1991) 19.
7. Kenneth Norrie, Richard Simeon, and Mark Krasnick, *Federalism and the Economic Union in Canada,* vol. 59 (Toronto: University of Toronto Press in co-operation with the Macdonald Royal Commission, 1986), 221.
8. Wayne R. Thirsk, "Interprovincial Trade and the Welfare Effects of Marketing Boards," in *Perspectives on the Canadian Economic Union,* vol. 60, ed. Mark Krasnick (Toronto: University of Toronto Press in co-operation with the Royal Commission on the Economic Union and Development Prospects for Canada, 1986), 26; Nola Silzer and Mark Krasnick, "The Free Flow of Goods in the Canadian Economic Union," in *Perspectives on the Canadian Economic Union,* vol. 60, ed. Mark Krasnick (Toronto: University of Toronto Press in co-operation with the Royal Commission on the Economic Union and Development Prospects for Canada, 1986), 157; John Whalley and Irene Trella, *Regional Aspects of Confederation,* vol. 68 (Toronto: University of Toronto Press in co-operation with the Royal Commission on the Economic Union and Development Prospects for Canada, 1986), 165.
9. Whalley and Trella, *Regional Aspects of Confederation,* 61, 126.
10. Tim Hazeldine, "Why do the free trade gain numbers differ so much? The role of industrial organization in general equilibrium," *Canadian Journal of Economics* 23, no.4 (1990): 791–806.
11. David J. Richardson, "Empirical Research on Trade Liberalisation with Imperfect Competition: A Survey," *OECD Economic Studies* no. 12 (1989).
12. Ibid., 9.
13. *Canadian Federalism and Economic Union,* 22.
14. Ibid., 1, 28, 33–35.
15. Ibid., 17.

16. McCraken, M. C., "Maritime Economic Integration — The External Environment," notes for an address to the Atlantic Provinces Economic Council Annual Meeting, 10 June 1991.
17. Michael Bradfield, *The Free Trade Claims: Smoke and Mirrors* (Ottawa: Canadian Centre for Policy Alternatives, October 1988).
18. *Canadian Federalism and Economic Union*, 27, 28.

Chapter Ten

1. A. M. Honore, "Ownership" in A. G. Guest, ed., *Oxford Essays in Jurisprudence* (London: Oxford University Press, 1961).
2. George Bernard Shaw, *The Intelligent Woman's Guide to Socialism, Capitalism, Sovietism & Fascism* (London: Constable & Co., 1928), 102.
3. For a discussion of some of these cases see Walter Tarnopolsky, *Discrimination and the Law* (Don Mills: De Boo, 1985), Chaps. 1 and 2.
4. Ibid.
5. Section 32 of the Charter has been interpreted by the Supreme Court of Canada as imposing Charter duties only on 'public,' not 'private,' entities: *R.W.D.S.U. v. Dolphin Delivery* [1986] 2 S.C.R. 573. 'Private' entities, including large corporations, have been granted Charter protection in numerous cases. See for example: *R. v. Big M Drug Mart* (1985), 18 D.L.R. (4th) 321 (S.C.C.); *Hunter et al. v. Southam Inc.* (1984), 11 D.L.R. (4th) 641 (S.C.C.).
6. "Misuse of court deplorable, Campbell says," *Vancouver Sun*, 26 September 1991, B9.
7. See Gerald Gunther, *Constitutional Law* (Mineola, New York: The Foundation Press, 1985), Chap. 8.
8. *Reference Re s. 94(2) of the Motor Vehicle Act* (1985), 24 D.L.R. (4th) 536 (S.C.C.).
9. J. Bakan, "Constitutional Interpretation and Social Change: You Can't Always Get What You Want (Nor

What You Need)" (1991) 70 *Canadian Bar Review* 307, 316–17.

Chapter Eleven

1. *Shaping Canada's Future Together: Proposals*, (Ottawa: Supply and Services Canada, 1991), 6–8.
2. Ibid., 7.
3. Ibid., 8.
4. Frank Cassidy and Norman Dale have produced a speculative study of the interaction between native communities and natural resource policy in British Columbia, assuming the settlement of comprehensive land claims. they project three possible scenarios — "Partners in Development," "Allies and Adversaries," and "Homeland and Hinterland" — to analyze the implications of land-claim settlements, and the book illustrates many of the complexities associated with the reconciliation of native, government, and third-party interests. See Frank Cassidy and Norman Dale, *After Native Claims: The Implications of Comprehensive Claims Settlements for Natural Resources in British Columbia*, (Victoria: Institute for Research on Public Policy, 1988).
5. Briefly, the Indians of most of British Columbia, Quebec, and the territories have not entered into treaties with the government, and thus claim outstanding aboriginal rights over and title to their traditional lands. The current land-claims policy is set out in *In All Fairness: A Native Claims Policy*,(Ottawa: Department of Indian Affairs and Northern Development, 1981) and *Outstanding Business* (Ottawa: DIAND, 1983). For an overview of the current land-claims process as well as proposals for its reform, see Murray Coolican, *Living Treaties, Lasting Agreements: Reports of the Task Force to Review Comprehensive Claims Policy*, (Ottawa: DIAND, 1985).
6. For a history and an analysis of the current legal position of the Metis peoples of Canada, see Donald Purich, *The Metis* (Toronto: James Lorimer and Co., 1988).

7. Martin Dunn, *Access to Survival: A Perspective on Aboriginal Self-Government for the Constituency of the Native Council of Canada* (Kingston: Queen's Institute for Intergovernmental Relations, 1986), 63, footnote 1.
8. *Shaping Canada's Future Together*, 7.
9. Ibid., 8.
10. Ibid., 8–9.
11. Quoted in *The Globe and Mail*, 26 September 1991, A6.
12. *The Globe and Mail*, 22 October 1991, A2. On October 31, the day the Assembly of First Nations Circle on the Constitution began its "parallel process" hearings in Hull, Québec, the AFN published a full-page advertisement in *The Globe and Mail* (A5) which spoke of broken promises and broken trust, and which quoted Mercredi as follows: "The self-government proposal is a hoax. It is designed to fool Canadians and secure a deal at the expense of all aboriginal peoples."
13. *Shaping Canada's Future Together*, 9.
14. Ibid., 7.
15. For elaboration of this position by various aboriginal leaders, see the essays in M. Boldt and J. A. Long, *The Quest for Justice: Aboriginal Peoples and Aboriginal Rights*. (Toronto: University of Toronto Press, 1985).
16. See for example, *Calder v. Attorney General of British Columbia*, [1973] 34 D.L.R. (3d) 145; *Guerin v. the Queen*, [1984] 6 W.W.R. 495; *Simon v. the Queen*, [1985] 2 S.C.R. 387; *R. v. Sioui*, [1990] 1 S.C.R. 1025; and *Sparrow v. the Queen*, S.C.C. 20311, 31 May 1990. For an excellent discussion of aboriginal rights case law, see Brian Slattery, "Understanding Aboriginal Rights," *Canadian Bar Review* 66 (1987).
17. For an analysis of major Supreme Court decisions on aboriginal rights, and particularly the recent set-backs in the *Horseman, Bear Island* and *Delgamuukw* decisions, see C. R. Jhappan, "Natural Rights v. Legal Positivism: New Principles and Tests in Aboriginal Rights Jurisprudence," October 1991, forthcoming publication.

18. For an analysis of the issues of jurisdiction, citizenship, policy making, service production and delivery, and financing, see Frank Cassidy and Robert Bish, *Indian Government: Its Meaning in Practice* (Victoria: Institute for Research on Public Policy, 1989). Alternatively, see the series on aboriginal self-government produced by Queen's University Press: David Hawkes, *Negotiating Aboriginal Self-Government (1985); C. E. S. Franks, Public Administration Questions Relating to Aboriginal Self-Government* (1986); E. J. Peters, *Aboriginal Self-Government Arrangements in Canada* (1987); and D. Boisvert, *Forms of Aboriginal Self-Government* (1986).
19. This explanation was offered by the Minister of Constitutional Affairs, Joe Clark, in his address to the First Nations Constitutional Circle, Museum of Civilization, Hull, Québec, October 31, 1991. Certainly, Mr. Mercredi's warning that native people may "secede" from Canada if the inherent right is not enshrined has done nothing to disabuse the government of this fear.
20. For example, Chief Billy Two Rivers of the Kahnawake Mohawk Council said: "The Haudenosaunee Six Nations Confederacy have no desire to separate from Canada, since the Confederacy have never been part of Canada ... [The] new constitution will have no jurisdictional authority within our territories or over our people. Our people are citizens of our nation and do not seek citizenship within the nation of Canada." See First Ministers Conference, unofficial verbatim transcript, (Ottawa: March 8–9, 1984), 256–257.
21. For a discussion and analysis of various assertions of sovereignty and jurisdiction, see C. Radha Jhappan, "Indian Symbolic Politics: The Double-Edged Sword of Publicity," *Canadian Ethnic Studies* XXII, 3 (1990): 19–39.
22. *Shaping Canada's Future Together*, 8.
23. The exception is the Sechelt model in British Columbia, which has been characterized as nothing more than a

municipal form of government and which is not the preferred model of the major aboriginal organizations, in any case. For a description of the Sechelt model, see Frank Cassidy and Robert Bish, *Indian Government: Its Meaning in Practice* (Victoria: Institute for Research on Public Policy, 1989), Chapter 7.

24. *The Globe and Mail*, 9 October 1991, A5.
25. Ibid.

Chapter Twelve

1. Canada, *Shaping Canada's Future Together: Proposals* (Ottawa: Supply and Services, 1991), 1.
2. Statistics Canada, *Women in Canada: A Statistical Report* (Ottawa: Supply and Services Canada, 1990), 77.
3. Ibid., x.
4. Gwen Brodsky and Shelagh Day write: "Women as a group are poorer than men. They work in ill-paid female ghettoes, they do more part-time work, they have fewer job protections and less access to unionization, benefits and pensions. Their gender determines the work they do and the pay they receive ... Women of colour work in environments with the least legal and union protections ... and women with disabilities are chronically unemployed or underemployed." See *Canadian Charter Equality Rights for Women: One Step Forward or Two Steps Back* (Ottawa: Canadian Advisory Council on the Status of Women, 1989), 11.
5. Statistics Canada, viii.
6. National Action Committee on the Status of Women, *NAC Response to Federal Constitution Proposals* (25 October 1991).
7. Ibid., 5.
8. In 1982, through the lobbying efforts of women's organizations, the general equality rights section in the Charter, section 15, was strengthened, and through the work of women in and beyond these groups, a new section entrenching sexual equality, section 28, was added. Section 15 did not come into effect until April

17, 1985. See Penny Kome, *The Taking of 28: Women Challenge the Constitution* (Toronto: Women's Press, 1983); Chaviva Hosek, "Women in the Constitutional Process," in *And No One Cheered,* eds. Keith Banting and Richard Simeon (Toronto: Methuen, 1983); Chaviva Hosek, "How Women Fought for Equality," in *Women and Men: Interdisciplinary Readings on Gender* ed. Greta Hoffman Nemiroff (Toronto: Fitzhenry and Whiteside, 1987); Sandra Burt, "The Charter of Rights and the Ad Hoc Lobby: The Limits of Success," *Atlantis* 14:1 (Fall 1988) 74–81.

9. See Brodsky and Day, passim.
10. Ontario, Ministry of Intergovernmental Affairs, *A Canadian Social Charter: Making Our Shared Values Stronger* (September 1991).
11. Chantal Maille, *Primed for Power: Women in Canadian Politics* (Ottawa: Canadian Advisory Council on the Status of Women, 1990).
12. A. Anne McLellan, *Women and the Process of Constitutional Reform* (Edmonton: Alberta Advisory Council on Women's Issues, 1991), 40.
13. See Banting's discussion of changes to the spending power in the Meech Lake Accord. K.G. Banting, "Federalism, Social Reform and the Spending Power," *Canadian Public Policy* 14 Supplement, (1988) 81–92.

Chapter Thirteen

1. C. B. Macpherson, ed., *Property: Mainstream and Critical Positions* (Toronto: University of Toronto Press, 1978).
2. Edmund Burke, *Reflections on the Revolution in France* (Middlesex: Penguin Books, 1969), 292.
3. David P. Shugarman, "Ideology and the Charter," in *Federalism and Political Community: Essays in Honour of Donald Smiley, ed. David P. Shugarman and Reg Whitaker (Peterborough: Broadview Press, 1989).*
4. Seymour Wilson, "What Legacy? The Nielson Task Force Program Review," in *How Ottawa Spends 1988–89,*

ed. Katherine Graham (Ottawa: Carleton University Press, 1988).

5. J. S. Mill, *Utilitarianism, On Liberty and Considerations on Representative Government,* ed. H. B. Acton (London: J. M. Dent & Sons, 1984), 55.
6. Persuasively argued treatments of the erroneous distinction between negative and positive rights and between social and political rights are found in Joèl Fineberg, *Rights, Justice and the Bounds of Liberty* (Princeton: Princeton University Press, 1980); C. Michael MacMillan, "Social versus Political Rights," *Canadian Journal of Political Science* 19, no. 2 (June 1986): 283–304; Henry Shue, *Basic Rights: Subsistance, Affluence and U. S. Foreign Policy* (Princeton: Princeton University Press, 1980).
7. Shue, *Basic Rights,* 22–27.
8. Sheldon Wolin, "Contract and Birthright," *Political Theory* 14, no. 2 (May 1986): 181.

Chapter Fourteen

1. For a fascinating discussion of the roots of such demands, see David Layton, *Populism and Democratic Thought in the Canadian Prairies, 1910–1945* (Toronto: University of Toronto Press, 1990).
2. Andrew Heard, *Canadian Constitutional Conventions: The Marriage of Law and Politics* (Toronto: Oxford University Press, 1991).
3. The government's authority to legislate is checked by federalism (i.e., the federal government cannot legislate in areas of provincial jurisdiction) and by the courts, especially since the adoption of the Charter of Rights and Freedoms.
4. On party discipline in Canada compared to other parliamentary systems, see the discussion in C. E. S. Franks, *The Parliament of Canada* (Toronto: University of Toronto Press, 1987).

5. B. Galligan, "An Elected Senate for Canada: The Australian Model," *Journal of Canadian Studies* 20, no. 4 (Winter 1985–86).
6. On recent reforms to the House, see *Parliamentary Internship Program, House of Commons Reform* (Ottawa: Carleton University, 1991).
7. *Shaping Canada's Future Together: Proposals* (Ottawa: Supply and Services, 1991), 16.
8. On the effect of the first-past-the post system on Canadian parties, see Alan Cairns, "The Electoral System and the Party System in Canada, 1921–1965," in *Constitution, Government and Society in Canada: Selected Essays by Alan Cairns*, Douglas E. Williams, ed. (Toronto: McClelland and Stewart, 1988) 111–140.
9. On corporate and interest-group donations to the Liberal and Conservative parties, see W. T. Stanbury, *Business-Government Relations in Canada: Grappling with Leviathan* (Scarborough, Ont.: Nelson, 1988), 440–59. On third-party spending during the 1988 campaign, see Nick Fillmore, "The Big Oink," *This Magazine* (March/April 1989).

Further Reading

Documents

Assembly of First Nations. *First Nations and the Constitution: Discussion Paper.* Ottawa: October 18, 1991.

Business Council on National Issues. *Canada and the 21st Century: Towards a More Effective Federalism and a Stronger Economy.* Ottawa: April 26, 1991.

Canada. *Canadian Federalism and Economic Union: Partnership for Prosperity.* Ottawa: Supply and Services, 1991.

Canada. Federal-Provincial Relations Office. *Amending the Constitution of Canada: A Discussion Paper.* Ottawa: Supply and Services, 1990.

Canada. *Shaping Canada's Future Together: Proposals.* Ottawa: Supply and Services, 1991.

Fidler, Richard, trans. and ed. *Canada Adieu? Québec Debates Its Future [Bélanger-Campeau Report].* Halifax: Institute for Research on Public Policy, 1991.

Liberal Party of Québec, Constitutional Committee. *A Québec Free to Choose [Allaire Report].* Québec City, 1991.

National Action Committee on the Status of Women. *NAC Response to Federal Constitutional Proposals.* Ottawa: October 25, 1991.

Ontario. Ministry of Intergovernmental Affairs. *A Canadian Social Charter: Making Our Shared Values Stronger.* Toronto: September 1991.

Québec. Commission on the Political and Constitutional Future of Québec. *The Political and Constitutional Future of Québec.* St-Romuald: Imprimerie St-Romuald, 1991.

Secondary Sources

Cairns, Alan. *Disruptions: Constitutional Struggles from the Charter to Meech.* Toronto: McClelland and Stewart, 1991.

Canadian Centre for Policy Alternatives. *Briefing Notes on the Constitution*. Ottawa: October, 1991.

McRoberts, Kenneth. *Québec: Social Change and Political Crisis*. 3rd ed. Toronto: McClelland and Stewart, 1988.

Milne, David. *The Canadian Constitution*. Revised ed. Toronto: Lorimer, 1991.

Network on the Constitution. *The Network* (newsletter). University of Ottawa, Department of Philosophy.

Ponting, J.R. *Arduous Journey: Canadian Indians and Decolonization*. Toronto: McClelland and Stewart, 1986.

Shugarman, David P., and Reg Whitaker, eds. *Federalism and Political Community: Essays in Honour of Donald Smiley*. Peterborough: Broadview Press, 1989.

Simeon, Richard, and Ian Robinson. *State, Society and the Development of Canadian Federalism*. Toronto: University of Toronto Press, 1990.

Swinton, K. E., and C. J. Rogerson. *Competing Constitutional Visions: The Meech Lake Accord*. Toronto: Carswell, 1988.

Young, Robert, ed. *Confederation in Crisis*. Toronto: Lorimer, 1991.

List of Contributors

Joel Bakan is a member of the Faculty of Law, University of British Columbia.

Michael Bradfield is a member of the Economics Department, Dalhousie University.

Duncan Cameron is editor of *The Canadian Forum*. He is a member of the Political Science Department, University of Ottawa.

Alexandra Dobrowolsky is a graduate student in the Political Science Department, Carleton University.

François Houle is a member of the Political Science Department, University of Ottawa.

Andrew Jackson is a director of the Canadian Centre for Policy Alternatives.

Jane Jenson is a member of the Political Science Department, Carleton University.

Radha Jhappan is a member of the Political Science Department, Carleton University.

A. W. Johnson is Professor Emeritus of Political Science at the University of Toronto and a former senior public servant in the governments of Saskatchewan and Canada.

Philip Resnick is a member of the Department of Political Science, University of British Columbia.

François Rocher is a member of the Political Science Department, Carleton University.

George Ross is Visiting Professor of Political Economy, Carleton University, and Senior Research Associate of the Center for European Studies, Harvard University.

David Schneiderman is Executive Director of the Centre for Constitutional Studies at the University of Alberta.

David P. Shugarman is a member of the Political Science Department, York University.

Miriam Smith is a member of the Political Science Department, Carleton University.

John D. Whyte is Dean of the Faculty of Law, Queen's University.

Index